Get Directions:

A Career as a Physicia

"A road map for a successful career begins in high school but can start from anywhere."

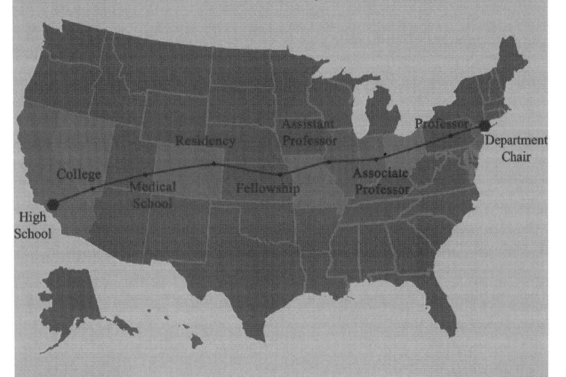

Current Location	High School
	College
	Medical School
	Residency and beyond

Get Directions

Richard Lee, MD, MBA

ISBN: 0692245405
ISBN-13: 9780692245408

Acknowledgements

That so many people have contributed to this book still amazes me. Since it is really a collection of experiences of my life and the lives of others, you could say that everyone I ever met contributed. But I will try to be more specific. First and foremost are my beautiful wife Michelle and our lovely daughters Geneva and Grace. Without them, I am nothing. Michelle has supported me during the most difficult times of my career. She is truly my soul mate. Without my parents, Richard and Barbara Pepelea, my sister Liz, my brother Mark and his wife Lisa—I would not be alive or the same.

My friends with whom I "pitched quarters" who always believed I would move on "from the corner" and selflessly encouraged it, especially Joe Musillami, Mark Stolfo and Tony Cerasualo. In high school, Bob Brennan, Tim Condon and Ted Hosty, taught me how to enjoy myself. In college, Drs. Vinky Chadha, Mike Safir, Malcolm Bilamoria and Pat Geraghty, as well as John Hussey got me through intact. In medical school, Drs. Michael Hochman and Vadim Gelman became lifelong best friends, advisors and even contributors to this book; their insights to the private practice section were critical. We still have many things in common, most of all having wives—still our first—who are better than we deserve. Residency is a decade-long blur, but Dr. Richard Prinz, Dr. William Gay, Dr. Richard Schuessler, Dr. Marc Moon, Dr. James Tweddle, Dr. Gordon Olinger, Dr. Patrick McCarthy, Dr. Joseph Sabik, and Dr. Delos Cosgrove truly inspired me to become the best physician I could be. They have continued to mentor and inspire me throughout my career.

In addition to the people I have mentioned, many friends have also contributed to this book by offering different perspectives and valuable substance. This includes Dr. John Ikonomides, who lent me his material on a successful academic career; and Dr. John Morley, Dr. Adrian DiBisceglie, Dr. Daniel Enter, Dr. Rishi Menon, Xiaoying Lou, Donna Staat, Nick Teodoro and my wife, who were all kind enough to share their perspectives. I am glad that they were able to give the readers advice beyond my own. Lynnda Greene gave invaluable editing and writing support, and made this worthy of reading. Ellen Sandor and Diana Torres brought it to life with their illustrations. Circling back to the beginning, I am indebted to Michael Yensel, who started Camp Cardiac and Camp Neuro with me and first proposed the idea for this book. He felt that as our camps expanded across the country, and I would no longer be able to meet with all the high school and medical students involved, a book would be a great way to still give them advice. I am sure there are many individuals who have been left out. For that I apologize; please remind me and you will be included in future editions. However, at the end of the day, *Get Directions* is really designed to offer counsel to all the students that follow us; we truly hope this book helps you achieve more than we have.

The most important contributors are our patients. Without them, there would be no reason to encourage others to enter the field. To all of you, please know we who are privileged to provide care for you are eternally grateful.

"If I have seen farther, it is because I have stood on the shoulders of giants." Bernard of Chartes, modified by Sir Isaac Newton.

Preface

Many paths can lead to successful careers in medicine. As with travel to any destination, some routes are direct and fast, and some are circuitous and slow depending on where and when you start. However, almost all of them proceed in one direction. If you are anywhere in the continental United States and your eventual destination is New York City, there are an infinite number of ways to get there; however, eventually, THEY ALL HEAD EAST.

The best decision I ever made was to pursue a career in medicine. Once I arrived, I discovered that the cliché was true: it is a privilege to practice medicine. I feel fortunate to have what most would consider a successful career; the rewards are beyond description. However looking back, I'm able to see that much of my success was accidental. When I started out, there was no road map showing how to arrive, no itinerary explaining the best routes, the most valuable stops. I couldn't just search the Internet for directions, and I couldn't rely on counselors, most of whom did not know enough to help. In fact, a great deal of advice I have received was bad and even harmful. Much of what I learned was by way by trial and error—mostly error.

This book is an attempt to help provide a map to a successful career in medicine as a physician. It identifies the major destinations or stops along the way, as well as various entry points and detours. It is not scientific or measured. Rather, it comes from personal reflections from my career and those of my wife, my peers, my mentors and mentees. It builds on my decade of experience in the medical school admission process, in running a residency program as either associate or program director, and on my privilege of working on national committees and journal editorial boards. But in the end, it is just advice. Take all of it, some of it—or leave it. Only you can and should be the judge of whether or not it applies to you.

The path to medical school really does start in high school. While you will encounter many obstacles, diversions and detours, you'll find they usually enrich the experience. Similarly, although medical specialties vary in their focus and intensity, they share more similarities than differences in the degree of success and reward they offer. "Get Directions" is an attempt to create a useful guide in a format similar to many of the internet tools we use to reach a destination. You can start at several points, and even get off track and be re-routed.

The following pages outline a path for a successful career in medicine. We share good and bad experiences, and describe options for those who start on the path from different places. Many readers will find themselves already at different points on the path; they should feel free to read only those sections that apply to them. At the end of several sections readers will find alternate perspectives from other people on the path. I can't begin to describe how fortunate I feel to have a career in medicine and only hope to be able to help others receive that gift. Looking back over my career, I realize that there were several points at which I could have left the path with irreversible consequences, and not realized my dream. If I'd had just a little help, or a tool to "Get Directions," I would have avoided those treacherous areas. My goal in writing this book is to help a few others find and stay on the right path. It is the only thanks I can offer to a field that has given me more than I can ever return.

Current Location

Get Directions: Life Path

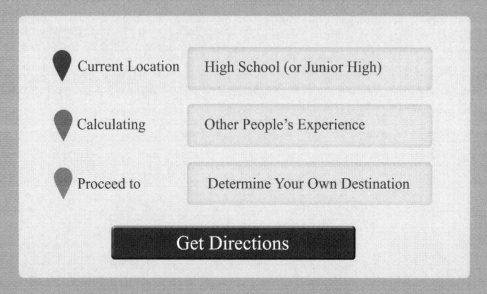

Current Location — High School (or Junior High)

Calculating — Other People's Experience

Proceed to — Determine Your Own Destination

Get Directions

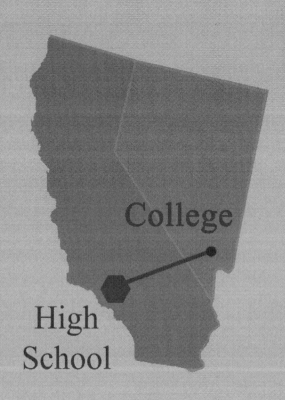

College

High School

Determine Your Destination

"Start from the end, *not* the beginning: determine the end destination"

For me, neither the path nor the destination was clear. I grew up in a lower middle class neighborhood that did not value education. The ultimate goal was to have a Cadillac or Lincoln Continental. A car like a Porsche or Mercedes seemed above us and thus was actually of no interest. My parents made a good decision to send me to Fenwick, a private all-boys Catholic high school in another suburb, where a greater emphasis on education promoted the expectation that all graduates would attend college. In those days, the threat of physical punishment, a rare occurrence, was highly effective in ensuring that when you were asked where you were going to college, you had an answer. If not, you would never make that mistake or sit down again.

My first useful insight into a life path began during my freshman year of high school. I was "pitching quarters" outside of Thomas Jefferson Grammar School with my neighborhood friends, one of whom attended Fenwick, and all of whom were of Italian-American descent. The stereotypes are quite frequently true. The amount of "Italian blood" was critical to membership in the group. The leaders' names all ended in "o" or "i," and most nicknames ended in "y" or "ie." Since I could boast only 25 percent "pure" blood, I was fortunate just to be in the pack. We were deep in a heated discussion about what kind of Cadillac we were going to have and what type of job we were going to have to get to pay for it when Bobby Rossano made a stunning declaration. "Ricky Lee's not going to have a Cadillac," he said. "He is going to be a fancy doctor, like a heart surgeon or something, and drive by us in a Porsche or Mercedes while we are still here pitching quarters."

The outburst made me think. Was that possible? What would it take to be a doctor, even a heart surgeon? I was sure that there were plenty of physicians who started out just like me, pitching quarters outside of a grammar school at some point in their lives. Why did they want to become a doctor, and how and when did they know? What decisions did they make along the way? Most importantly, what aspects of their work made them believe their lives were worth living?

I decided that day to start looking at the end of my life and how I wanted it to have been. I immediately began interviewing different people and asking them about their life choices, a practice I still continue. I wanted to make sure that at the end of my life, I was not full of regret in my choice of job or what I had done. So of everyone I have met since then, I ask one recurrent question: "What is the most rewarding aspect of your job?"

I would encourage you to do the same. When asked the question, "What do you want to be when you get older?" many children and young adults answer the question "A doctor". No one really stops to answer the questions "Why?" and "How do you know?" It is okay to answer "A doctor" but it makes sense to look at the entire span of a career and try to figure out what you want to get out of it. Even though you will change your mind or have doubts, even though you may recognize that you are very young and have plenty of time to "figure it out," take a small break today to figure out what you think you want to get out of your life. You may need to do it again tomorrow and the answer may be different. You are not alone. There are roughly 20,000 high schools in the USA, according to the National High School Center. You are one of about 15 million young adults trying to figure it out. However, if you have a plan, you are more likely than the other 14,999,999 students to achieve your goal, even if that goal is to have more fun than any other person that has ever lived. "The man (or woman) with the plan always wins," as the saying goes. However, before you make a personal roadmap to identify the "next stop," you should have an idea in mind of where you want to end up.

Get Directions: Life Path

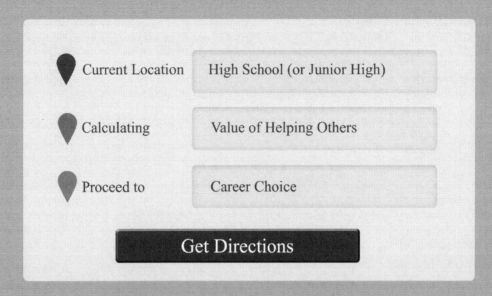

Current Location — High School (or Junior High)

Calculating — Value of Helping Others

Proceed to — Career Choice

Get Directions

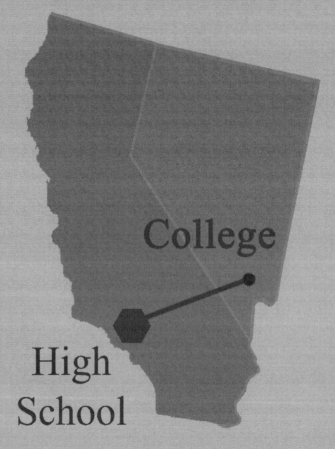

College

High
School

Career Choice

"Only go into medicine for the right reason: to help others. Only choose *not* to go into medicine for the right reason: to help others (differently)."

I have found that when you ask the majority of people what they like about their job, it always relates to service part of their job, the part that helps other people.

One of the first people I approached with my question in high school was my dad. A vice-president for a small auto insurance company, he had spent his lifetime in the field, working long hours and giving it his best. His work ethic continues to set "the bar" for me to reach.

"Dad, what do you find most rewarding about your job?" I asked, expecting to hear that insurance made people safer, or that he enjoyed the authority he yielded, etc.

He thought about this deeply for a while; but his answer, when it came, surprised me. "I feel good about creating jobs and enabling my employees to provide for their families."

I couldn't believe it. The most important aspect of his countless hours of insurance work was the fact that he was helping others around him. He took pride in the impact he made on the families of his employees.

Next I asked my great-grandmother, who was nearly 100 years old. "Grandma, what did you enjoy most in your life?"

"I think I made a difference in the lives of my family and friends," she answered. "Your uncles and aunts grew up in the hard times of the Great Depression. It was tough to keep our families and friends together, but we did. Now everyone has jobs or is retired and we all made it through. I am pretty sure we would have lost some of us if I hadn't been around." Again, it seemed like a very similar answer. She *valued* the impact she made on those around her.

I have asked this question of countless individuals walking life paths as different as they are diverse. Whether billionaire or housekeeper, most people's responses are strikingly similar for the degree of gratification they get from helping others. Ultimately, the one thing they valued above all in their lives was the impact that they have had on those around them.

To me, medicine seemed like the easiest way to get that reward. You wouldn't have to make a billion dollars to hold charity events and you wouldn't have to endure something you didn't enjoy. You could make a living helping others. Now that is a great deal! Medicine is not for everyone, and there are many ways to help people. No matter what path you choose, however, make sure some facet of the work you do allows you to better the lives of those around you.

A billionaire I know confirmed this in a recent conversation. "Rick, my only limit is my time," he said. "What really motivates me and what I spend my time on is the charity work our organizations do with underprivileged kids. I think we are really making a difference." I am confident that this is a near universal opinion.

On the other hand, I have met several disgruntled physicians at earlier stages of their careers. Many of them had lost their way. In some cases they seemed to have chosen their "work to live," a medical career as a lifestyle. This was their mistake. You will work hard in any aspect of medicine. You will in all likelihood not become rich. I was 45 years old before I could pay off my school loans. If you enter the field of medicine for any other reason than helping others, you will be disappointed. However, if you recognize at the end of the day, at the end of your life, that what you have done for others will define who you are and the footprint you have left behind, then you'll find there is NO other career that can give you more than a career in medicine. If your passion is not medicine, follow a different path, but make sure that you can find a way to help others.

I can relate thousands of examples of a medical career's rewards, but I will share one of particular meaning to me. Dr. B. is an eye doctor with a beautiful wife and three young children. He treats and saves the sight of hundreds of patients each year. Five years ago he learned he had an ascending aortic dissection. This is a very dangerous condition where the aorta—the main pipe leading "out" from your heart to your body—tears, allowing some of the blood to go between the layers of the tube instead of to the center. When this occurs, the aortic wall weakens. In many cases it ruptures within a few hours of the onset of pain, and the patient dies.

When Dr. B. came to me, I operated emergently, replaced the aorta with an artificial tube, and he was back to work in a few weeks. I am always pleased when I save someone's life, but usually they move on with their lives and I move on to the next patient. However each year on Father's Day, Dr. B's wife and children send me a card thanking me for another year with their dad. It brings tears of joy to my eyes just thinking about it. Dr. B usually sends me a note on the "anniversary" of his operation, reminding me of how many more patients he has been able to help. I remind him that this privilege, this feeling that I made a difference, is what I live for. I am the one who is thankful. Nothing else in life, no other job, can give you a better experience or more meaning.

Get Directions: Medical Career

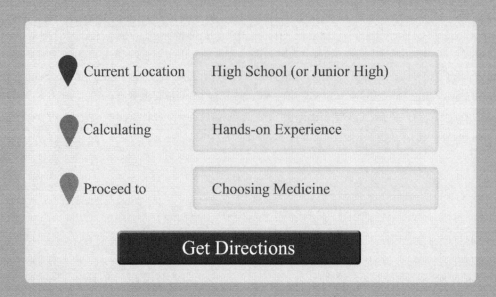

Current Location	High School (or Junior High)
Calculating	Hands-on Experience
Proceed to	Choosing Medicine

Get Directions

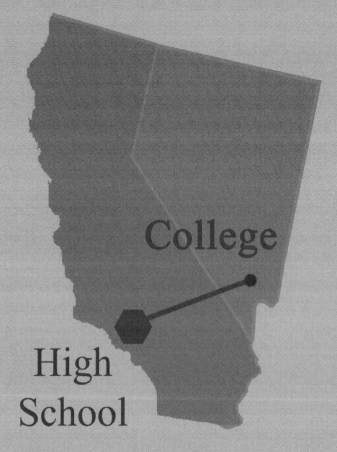

College

High School

Choosing Medicine

"I am in high school and have decided that I want to help others. How do I find out if I want to go into medicine?"

I often meet high school students who are struggling with this question. This is the easy part. I ask them, "What do you like to do, what are your hobbies?" They usually look at me oddly and then respectfully respond with an answer related to sports, dance, entertainment, etc. Then I ask, "How did you find out that you liked it?"

The response is the same: "I tried it."

Try it! Obviously you can't just try heart surgery or read X-rays, but you can *talk* to people who do it and ask them about their job. Recognize that there are many careers in medicine. Not everyone wants to be a doctor. My mom had a *great* career as a nurse. You can be a physician assistant, a hospital administrator, a pharmacist, an x-ray technician, a dietitian, a transporter or any one of a myriad of other health professionals who help people. Since about 18 percent of the economy is spent on health care, I guarantee that you and your family and friends know at least one, and probably several, people who work in the health care field. Certainly someone in your family has gone to a doctor or has gotten sick. Go to with them to their doctor's appointment or visit them in the hospital. Reach out to the health care professionals you meet and talk to them. Ask them about their jobs. If they don't do what you would like to know about, ask them if they can introduce you to someone who does.

I am surprised on a daily basis at how eager people in medicine are to help others interested in the field. I have never known a doctor who would not meet at least once with a high school student who was interested in his or her specialty. It is true that imitation is the greatest form of flattery. I am flattered when someone wants to know about what I do and I am happy to talk to them about it at the right time and place. But even if my time doesn't work out for you, someone else's will. Many high schools now offer mentorship programs for students interested in a variety of fields. Take advantage of these opportunities. Ask to shadow your pediatrician or family doctor for a day or two. Even if you are looking at a career outside of medicine, I am confident the inquiry will be warmly received.

Besides asking questions, you should try to get some hands-on experience, and fortunately you can find many different opportunities to do this. You can volunteer in a hospital or a doctor's office, apply for a summer job or internship, or attend a summer camp. I personally helped start "Camp Cardiac" and "Camp Neuro," two summer programs for high school students for that specific purpose. Several other opportunities, such as "mini med school" programs, are also available in many areas around the country. These are pretty easy to find on the Internet, and many offer scholarships and tuition assistance. I know this may seem overwhelming and you have a lot of things to do. However, you can find many opportunities to invest a little time in this decision. For example, you could spend one day a month or one week a summer learning something about medical careers—whether volunteering at a hospital or reaching out to a doctor you already know—as a first step. If you did both, by the end of your high school, you would have spent 76 days exploring a career! Even if you find out you don't like medicine, you can do the same thing in any field. My elder daughter is interested in politics. I have encouraged her to spend a little time volunteering on a campaign. If you want to explore law, meet and talk with a lawyer or judge or paralegal, etc. It really is not that hard to do and even a few days of experience can make a big difference.

An Alternative Perspective from a Student Entering Medical School

The importance of volunteering early in a medical setting

I volunteered at a hospital in high school because I needed the volunteer credit. While I was mildly interested in medicine at that point, I wasn't interested in *being* a doctor, because I didn't like the personalities of the ones I knew. In Phoenix, anyway, most doctors were in private practice, and seemed to me to be arrogant, focused solely on money and lifestyle—and that was just not me at all. But I ended up learning a lot from that first experience in a hospital setting.

Later in college, I began doing some research on campus to get a feeling for what it would be like to be a PhD in biochemistry. I also volunteered in a hospital and for the American Heart Association during this time. But it wasn't until my junior year in college that I finally made the decision to go into medicine. Through Dr. Lee I had the opportunity to go participate in a summer program at Northwestern, where he was working at the time—and that was the big turning point. Meeting so many doctors working academia, in research, in clinics and NGOs (non-Government organization), I realized medicine is a broad field, and that being a doctor means you can do all kinds of different things, not just one thing.

It really is a matter of exposure, because no one can tell you. You don't know what's possible unless you make an effort to enter that world and find out.

Get Directions: Choosing A Career

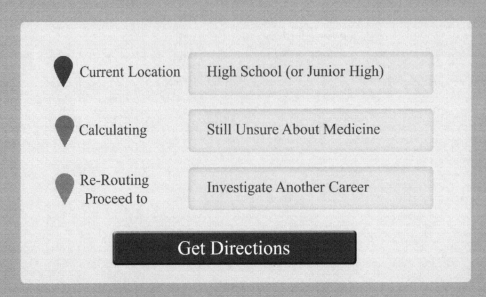

Current Location	High School (or Junior High)	
Calculating	Still Unsure About Medicine	
Re-Routing Proceed to	Investigate Another Career	

Get Directions

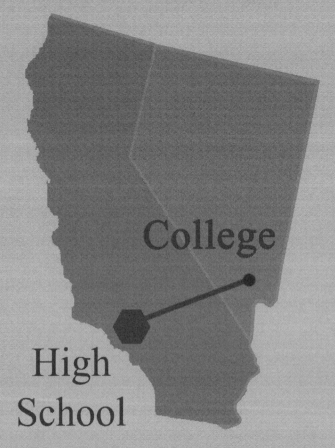

Unsure About Medicine

"I am in high school and I agree that I want to help others, but I STILL don't know if I want to go into medicine. What do I do?"

Just pick a different destination or even two. Try to shadow a veterinarian, or a lawyer or anything else. At this point in your life, you don't have to know; you just need to start. You'll be amazed at how much of what you learn starting down one path can apply to others. You can always change your mind. You may go down a different path and like it better, or decide that you want to return to medicine. It doesn't really matter at this point which path you try; you will benefit no matter what career you choose.

The analogy I give students is the following. Say you are in Chicago and want to go skiing in Colorado for spring break. The car is packed and you are driving. Halfway there, you find out that the snow has melted and the ski lifts are closed. No problem! You are halfway there, so why not continue? You can go to the resort and enjoy the spa; you can go Utah and ski there; or you can go on to California and enjoy the beach. The point is that you are much closer to all those options than if you were still sitting in Chicago saying, "Hmmm. I don't know if I want to go skiing or not. What should I do?"

For example, say you want to become a heart surgeon like me (excellent choice) and you follow the path outlined in the following chapters. You start out going in that direction (Colorado). You decide it is not for you and you want to do something else in health care (radiology, nursing, physical therapy=Utah). You are still much closer to your goal. Even if you decide to do something totally different (law, business=California), the steps you have taken—grades, ACT prep, even volunteering—will help you toward that path. It might not be direct or efficient, but that is not only okay, it is good. Nothing in life is really that direct. Letting your experience guide you is what life is all about.

Progressing through life is like steering a boat. You head out from shore in one direction, intending to reach a certain destination. Though an unexpected current may take you somewhere else entirely—the Spanish coast, say, instead of Greece—you're still moving. No matter where you end up, the journey will have been exciting and worthwhile for all the valuable experience gained along the way.

Just untie your boat from the dock and jump on board!

Get Directions: College Admission

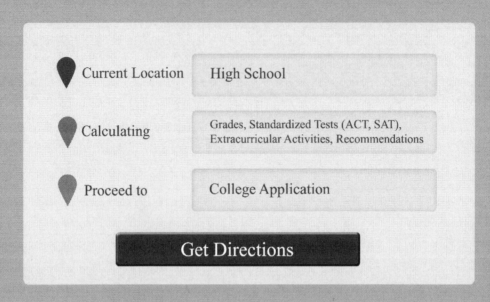

Current Location	High School
Calculating	Grades, Standardized Tests (ACT, SAT), Extracurricular Activities, Recommendations
Proceed to	College Application

Get Directions

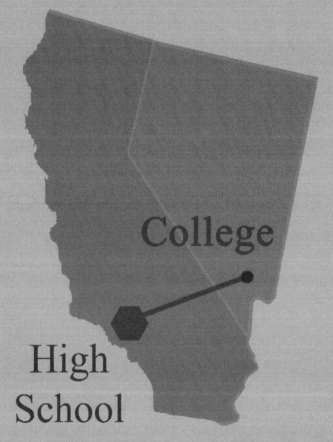

College

High School

Qualifications for College

"I am in high school and think I want to go into medicine. What next?"

Obviously, you need to go to college. No matter where you decide to go, the "transportation," or the "tickets" are the same: 1) grades; 2) standardized tests (ACT/SAT); 3) extracurricular activities; 4) recommendations/personal connections. Some of these components carry more weight than others, depending upon the school's preferences, which a little research will reveal.

Information on average scores that schools accept is readily available, for example. Additionally, I encourage you to reach out early not only to your high school counselors but also members of college admission committees, and ask them what you should be doing. Before you take or leave their advice, pretend that you are the one deciding on an admission and ask yourself, "What would I look for in an applicant?" The answer to that question can help you decide your next move along the path.

Below I provide my personal perspective on each of the "tickets."

Grades

4.0 (or "straight As") is the goal. Obviously, a 4.0 average is rarely achievable and needs to be balanced by your other activities, as well as fun. A few tips can help you, however.

1) Build a strong foundation. As part of this, challenge yourself, but don't *overchallenge* yourself. My daughter is facing this now. She is clearly an "overachiever" and prides herself on being ahead two years in math and language, like I was. However, I learned everything comes with a price. Often, "skipping" components hurts your foundation of fundamentals. Admission committees are slightly impressed when you get an "A" in an

advanced class, but are extremely disappointed in a "C" or worse. For the right individual, jumping ahead makes sense, but if you are "on the fence," staying in regular classes may give you a better foundation. You will have plenty of time to cover advanced concepts in college. In fact, with a more solid foundation you may be better prepared to excel later in life. Further, if you can balance your load by taking one or two "hard classes" at a time, it is generally easier to excel in all.

2) Try imagining that you are the college admissions officer reviewing your college application. When I "put myself in their shoes" and pretend that I am a college admissions officer reviewing hundreds or thousands of applications, I ask myself several questions. "How would I choose who to interview? How would I know whose AP class was really hard and whose was easy? Wouldn't it be easier to just take the person who got an A and did well on the standardized tests?" For me the answer is obvious. Yes, it would be easier to take the person who did well on the standardized test and got an A in every class. The test results allow me to compare all students by a single assessment tool. Clearly I can't know how hard or easy every class is in every school. A word of caution, however. I am not suggesting that you should take only easy classes; only that you balance them. The admissions committee will notice if you take all easy classes. You want your record to stand out, not your class schedule.

3) Incorporate a strong basic science foundation into your curricula. If you are serious about pre-med, taking science classes now will be very helpful in college when you repeat the material. Because I had a strong high school preparation, I found my freshman of college to be largely review—and that led me to make the first big mistake of my college career: I didn't study as if I were seeing the material for the first time. Though I could have easily gotten straight As, I opted to spend time working for spending money, rather than building on my knowledge and mastering the subjects. However, my foundation was strong enough that it could accommodate my early mistakes, which I made sure not to repeat.

4) Learn from your mistakes. It is okay if you stumble and get a bad grade or two; just be sure to use the experience as an opportunity to learn. Reflect earnestly on what you could have done differently to change that grade, or

18

at what points in the cycle you could have altered it. There will always be more than one way that you could have altered the outcome. The next time, it will be easier to identify and change before the final grade.

5) Ask for help early. Your teachers are resources. If you have a hard time with a subject, reach out for help before a test. If you have a bad test, go to the teacher immediately and ask for help. Be receptive to what they say. If they can't or don't help you, ask another student in your class or someone who has taken the subject before and done well. It is easier to prevent a bad grade than to make up for one. You should not be embarrassed to get help. You should be embarrassed if you need help and don't get it.

6) Set your expectations with the decision maker up front. Go to your teacher day one, or even before school starts and set the expectation. Obviously *no* teacher wants you to learn for a grade, or just work for an "A". However, they do want to help you learn. I would approach them and say, "I want to master this subject and get everything I can out of this class. I hope you can help me achieve this objective during the year. What can I do to maximize my experience?" If you are unhappy about a grade on an assignment, talk to the teacher but not about the grade. Focus instead on your efforts. "Clearly, I did not perform to my expectations. How can I improve?"

7) Remember you are the student. Even though you are smart, your teacher is grading you, not the other way around. It is your job to figure out what makes her or him tick, what their expectations are and how to exceed them. Arguing with them sometimes works in the short run, but it can come back to bite you when it comes to your applications, your letters of recommendation and your reputation.

8) Learn to take responsibility for your actions. This is very difficult and usually requires more age and maturity than most people ever achieve. However, many achieve it early on. You can only control your own actions. No one else's. If you did not get the result that you want, figure out what *you* can do differently. In the end, no one will be more invested in you— than you. So if you don't get the grade or the score you want, don't blame anyone else. Spend your time constructively, not destructively, and figure out what you can do next time.

Standardized Tests

These are the only means by which to really evaluate and compare individuals from different institutions. No matter how hard or easy a school is, the ACT and SAT offer the best opportunity for level comparison. Nationwide, the average ACT score is about a 21 and the average SAT score, including writing sample, is about a 1450. However, an average score will not get you into a top school. The highest score is 36 for the ACT and 2400 for the SAT. Obviously, the best score you can get will give you the best chance of attending a top school. It is really up to you. These tests rank as the first of many, many standardized tests that you will take throughout your career. And quite honestly, they are not even close to the hardest. Some students are naturally better at taking these tests than other students. Too bad! It is up to you to figure out how to do your best. It has been shown that many of these tests predict outcomes on future tests (MCAT, Step 1, etc.). Even if "your best" is not "good enough" for your next goal, it will nonetheless establish a pattern for reaching it. I do have a few hints, however, that can help you do your best.

1) Study like you mean it! When you prepare for these tests, make it blocked time for nothing else. No TV, no music, etc. They don't allow any distractions during the test, so avoid them when you study. Create an environment similar to the test setting every time you study, so it won't freak you out when the test comes. You will be used to it.

2) You can never start too early. Several students in my daughter's classes have been studying for these tests since the 6th grade. While we have chosen not go this route with our girls, but I expect those students to do better. Life is about balance. For example, we have chosen to allow our daughters to pursue other interests like athletics, but that is a choice. If your goal is to fully optimize the results on the standardized tests, it is never too early to begin.

3) Take a formal test prep class, but take it early. Data clearly indicate that test prep classes, such as those offered by Kaplan, have clearly made a difference in scores. Several such test preparation organizations exist, but I do not endorse any particular one. However, those students who do not take these classes are clearly at a disadvantage. I personally recommend starting the course in the summer of freshman year. There is plenty of time to find out where you stand and what you need to study along the way. If the materials are beyond your comprehension, that is okay. Just keep the books and study them when you start the subjects in school.

4) Study from the review books as a supplement as you are learning the material. That way, you will become familiar with the format of the subject for the test. Do not use it as a primary source, but clearly you can do additional questions and problems in real time as they relate to your classes.

5) Re-review the materials and take practice tests on weekends and breaks. Obviously, you will be very, very busy. It is hard to do. However, the materials are light. Bring a book to the swim meet and do some problems between events. Bring it in the car and do a few problems while you are waiting for your sibling to be done. The more you review the materials and the more times you work through the problems, the better prepared you will be.

6) Remember, the standardized tests don't test what you know, but what everyone should know. You may be years ahead of the subject on the tests and may have forgotten the material or gotten rusty. The only way to stay sharp is to practice. Again, this needs to be worked in with your other activities, but if you only do about 10% more than your peers, it will pay tremendous dividends.

7) If you perform below your expectations, you can retake the test. Don't take the test unless you are prepared, but *really* don't RE-TAKE the test unless you are prepared. One mistake is bad. Two is a pattern. Don't do exactly the same preparation for the second time and expect a different outcome. It won't be different. Reflect on what you did well and duplicate it. Reflect on what you did not do well on and change the strategy.

Extracurricular activities

There is no single option here and quite frankly, at this point in your life you should try many things. If you are planning a career in medicine, there are a few recommendations I have.

1) Choose an activity that you like and in which you excel. Many students choose athletics. This is a good choice for many reasons. However, I would recommend trying a sport that offers many scholarships. This information is readily available on the internet. For example if you are good at track but also participate in equestrian competitions and are about the same in each, figure out which receives more scholarships in colleges around the country. You may not be able to get a scholarship but if that skill is valued at a school, the value of your application increases. My daughter, for example, is

a competitive runner and swimmer. The seasons overlap and in reality, both are currently full year sports. She has gone to state competitions in each sport every year. However, she is more competitive in running than in swimming and performs at an all-state level. In her sophomore year, she chose to focus on running. It was a difficult but excellent choice. She has already received recruitment letters from colleges that value her skill. However, the activity can be drama, chess, or anything for which you have a passion.

2) At the same time, include an activity that relates to a medical career. It can be volunteering at a hospital or nursing home, shadowing a physician, or performing research in a lab. Ideally the activity, which need not be extensive, will include some patient contact. Whatever you choose, however, should start in high school. The experience will help keep you on the path or help you choose a new one. Either way, most individuals begin here.

3) Colleges often look for a component of "giving back," especially if you come from a background of privilege. It is important to recognize one's advantages and how they can help you relate to future patients or co-workers that may not have had it so easy. Volunteering at your church, for food drives or children's organizations, etc., all demonstrates sensitivity toward others and helps form your self-awareness.

4) If you come from an underrepresented group, participate in an organization unique to your background. Most admission committees, especially in medical school, value diversity. In fact, patients in underserved communities often prefer physicians from similar communities. However, students who may have a similar ethnicity may not have a similar background. For example, if you identify your background as "Hispanic" but don't speak Spanish, or identify yourself as "Native American" but don't know what tribe to which you belong, expect some increased scrutiny over your application.

5) Summers. This deserves their own category. Summers should not be squandered. Even if you spend part of the summer vacationing or having fun, choose the rest wisely. No matter how much you can make waiting tables or how tan you can get as a lifeguard (I did both), it would be better to get an experience valuable—even if unpaid—for your life path. Just try to make sure the experience is worthwhile. This is sometimes a tough sell for parents who wish to teach their kids the value of a dollar, or for young adults who want a car. However, saving a year's worth of potentially wasted

tuition (now about $50,000 a year) is more than most adults can make over a summer. For parents reading here, keep in mind this is the first of *many* opportunities for delayed gratification. Having watched many young professionals progress through their careers, I notice that the most successful in the long run are usually those capable of shooting for long term rather than immediate goals. That is a lesson more valuable than any summer job.

Personal Connections

While worrying about connections in high school may seem premature, this is actually a very good time to begin networking. Generally it is at this point that you will create many if not most of your opportunities. Currently grades and test scores count the most in the admissions process, but as the world grows smaller and more interconnected, they may not always carry so much weight. As jobs become more specialized and competition for fellowships and first positions more intense, *who* you know will become an increasingly important factor in building a career. This will be discussed extensively in later chapters, but I'd like to address it initially here, with a true story.

There was a high school student in Cleveland who decided that he wanted to be a heart surgeon. He went to a heart surgeon at the Cleveland Clinic and shadowed him. In college, during summer breaks, the student worked with the surgeon again. The surgeon became head of heart surgery. The student stayed in touch during medical school and residency, visiting intermittently. The heart surgeon eagerly provided advice and recommendations. At the end of training, the former high school student accepted a job at the Cleveland Clinic, the most prestigious cardiac institution in the country. The head of heart surgery continued to support the young surgeon's career in a way that can only occur over time.

You may be the type of person who will give the shirt off your back to a stranger. However, even if you are, you would likely be willing to share even more with a friend. Such close personal and professional relationships evolve over time and cannot occur with a single brief experience. Several similar experiences can lead to relationships that make a tremendous difference in the long term.

It is unlikely that you will be as lucky as the high school student above, but you never know. I have worked with many high school students over the years. I continue to support them. I may even hire one someday. If you start now, it will only help. However, there are other shorter term goals you can consider. For example, if you want to go to a specific college, reach out to someone on the admissions committee at that college. Not everyone will respond, but some will. Find out directly from them what you ought to be doing to get there. No one can give you better advice.

Get Directions: College Admission

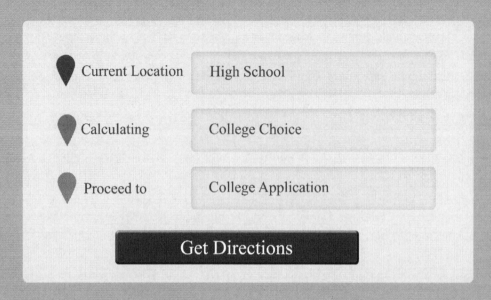

Current Location — High School

Calculating — College Choice

Proceed to — College Application

Get Directions

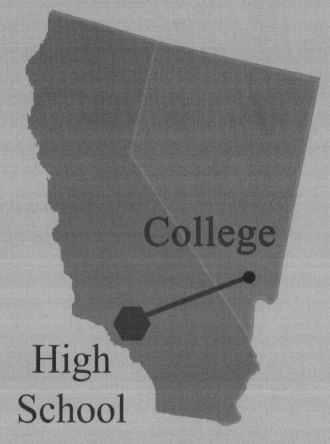

College

High School

Choosing a College

"Which college should I go to?"

This is a tough question, and is very individual, but I can give you my best advice.

1) Choose the college or university with the most name recognition. There are approximately 4,500 universities, colleges and junior colleges in the US. Among them are a lot of incredible schools ranging from large state universities to small "boutique" colleges that will provide terrific educations. However, you don't want to spend time explaining where you went to school every time you are asked. If you can answer "Harvard", or "Yale", no explanation is needed. I went to Northwestern. Many state schools, such as the universities of Michigan, Illinois, Wisconsin and California in Los Angeles, are excellent and offer high value name recognition. There is no single "right" school and I certainly did not have my choice of all the schools listed above. However if your decision is between a widely recognized school and one that most people have never heard of, choose the widely recognized school. Association with such a school will simplify your career path in many ways, not the least of which will be a dense alumni network that may help you later. At the very least, it is a conversation point and something you have in common. My wife went to the University of Wisconsin. We were recently out to dinner with some potential donors for my institution. As it happens, their daughter went to the University of Wisconsin, or "Madison," as most alumni refer to it, so they all spent at least 30 minutes reminiscing about the winters there. By contrast, comparable connections through smaller schools tend to decrease exponentially.

2) Choose a college with a track record for placement into your field. Most colleges track this type of information, but not all do and prying it out of them can be tough. Usually, they prefer to use non-quantitative phrases like "we have an excellent track record" or "most of our graduates who wish to attend medical school do so." You want the numbers. Get the percent of pre-med students who start pre-med and eventually go to medical school or at least the percent of applicants who applied to medical school and were accepted. If that does not work, try to get information from the medical schools you may wish to attend down the road (usually in the state you attended high school) and find out where their incoming freshmen students went to college. There won't be a great pattern, and some great schools that could be on the list may not be; but if the medical school you are interested in frequently accepts graduates of a particular college or university, I'd strongly suggest that you consider applying to those schools.

3) Choose a college that "feels" right to you. This is hard to quantify, as each school has its own personality. College is difficult and can be lonely if you don't know anyone. Try to pick one that makes you comfortable when you visit.

4) Be sensitive to price. Tuition is *expensive*. In its most recent survey of college pricing, the College Board reports that a "moderate" college budget for an in-state public school for the 2013–2014 academic year averaged $22,826. A moderate budget at a private college averaged $44,750. Roughly multiply that by 4 for each year for total cost. While scholarships are available, most students borrow to cover the cost. According to a Fidelity survey of 750 college graduates, between student loans, credit cards and family members, the average college graduate owes $35,200 in debt upon graduation. For private schools, the cost is substantially more. Even if your parents can pay, it would be better for them to help with medical school tuition, which is also very expensive. Only you can decide, but if you are choosing between two colleges that are close in all the categories above, but one is substantially less expensive, choose the less expensive school. Perhaps it offers a scholarship, or in the case of a state university, in-state tuition breaks. However, especially if you need to rely on loans, you may as well keep costs as low as possible. It will be a long time until you can pay those loans back and often the interest accrues during training.

5) Clearly this is a competitive process, so choose to apply to several different tiers of schools. There are so many excellent options that none need be a backup. Your first choice is the school in which you end up.

6) In the end, the decision is not critical. When you look at successful people in all career paths, there is no right or wrong choice. Only a right or wrong choice for you. If your initial choice turns out to be a mistake, a transfer to another school is always an option.

Get Directions: College Admission

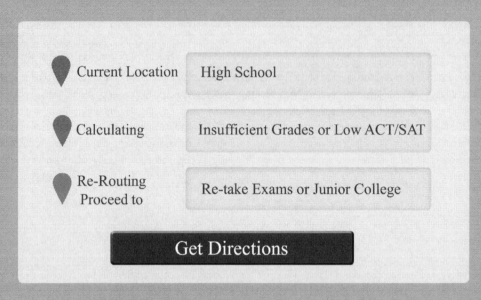

Current Location	High School
Calculating	Insufficient Grades or Low ACT/SAT
Re-Routing Proceed to	Re-take Exams or Junior College

Get Directions

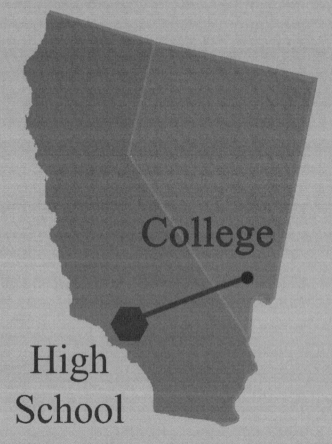

College

High School

Poor Grades or Low ACT/SAT

"My scores/grades weren't good enough to get into college."

Life is full of ups and downs; the trick is turning a down into an up. You will make many, many mistakes in your life. That's okay. It just means that you need to work a little harder than others to catch up.

Standardized Tests. You can take them again. It is not as good as getting a good score initially, but that is okay. I would only recommend that if you take them again, you do so only if you *know* you will get a better score. Overstudy! Make sure that your practice tests show a marked improvement. The last thing you want to do is decrease your score or even keep it exactly the same. You will be telling school admissions committees that the bad score was a "fluke." Prove it. If you cannot, take pride in the score and tell them that you are proud of it, as you worked hard for it and earned it. Tell them you wish it were higher, but you did your absolute best and that the score does not define you. However, you will have to prove it by getting great grades. If you do your best and yet you are denied admission to your dream school, go to a different one. There is always one that you can get into. Once there, start working on improving your ability to perform on standardized tests. There are many more to come.

GPA Remedies. A bad GPA is difficult to overcome. If it is too low to attend a four year school, the best option is to attend a junior or community college. While starting from this point may rack up a few more odds against you, it's important to recognize that many physicians and other successful people begin their journeys at community colleges, which are renowned for their ability to help students of all backgrounds get on track. Obviously a radical reformation of attitude and study habits will be required. Schoolwork needs to become the highest priority and you need to deliver on grades. One thing you can do, however, is analyze a given junior college's placements. If you see that a particular two year school often places students into a specific four year college, then that is a pattern that merits exploration. Often, the patterns are local, i.e. good local junior college councilors know one another. They know that transferring students tend to do well in certain four year schools, and those four year schools are more likely to accept students from a particular junior college.

If you cannot do well in a junior college, at this point, I would suggest that you consider looking at alternate careers in medicine. There are a number of careers beyond the scope of this book that include x-ray technicians, transporters, nursing and a host of others. Each requires some degree of training that, while rigorous, is less time-consuming than medical school. I recommend that you pursue one of those paths. Perhaps you are a late bloomer. If so, you can try for medical school again later. You have plenty of time. However, you do need to be able to perform well in school. Medical school is hard and requires a great deal of memorization and work. You must demonstrate sufficient performance in school to progress to that step.

Get Directions: Medical School Admission

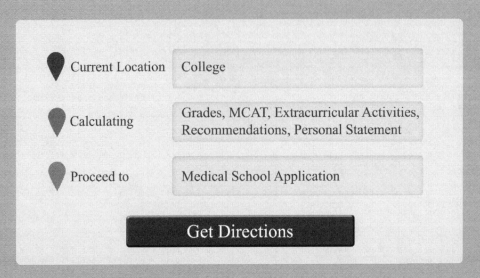

Current Location	College	
Calculating	Grades, MCAT, Extracurricular Activities, Recommendations, Personal Statement	
Proceed to	Medical School Application	

Get Directions

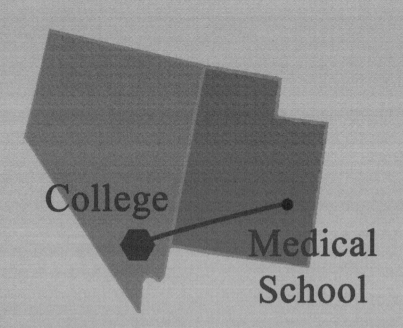

Qualifications for Medical School

"I am in a good four year college and want to go to medical school. What next?"

This is easy. Once again, start at the end of the next step (medical school admission) and work backwards. Virtually all admissions committees have a formula that, whether written or unwritten, is similar across all institutions. The formula would look something like this:

40% grade point average + 40% MCAT Score + 20% "other" = interview or denial

While each component is unique and merits an entire chapter, most schools set their own minimum requirements in creating their formulas. Thus a great MCAT can only partially make up for a weak GPA.

Once you decide to try to go into medical school it is critical that you focus on each component and work to optimize your score on each one. This work doesn't start "next year" or later, it starts the second you make the decision. Like the tortoise and the hare, you will end up at the same finish line, but you will be more likely to be successful if you pace yourself and do a little at a time rather than try to catch up all at once. The preparation you do now begins on the foundation you built in high school. If this is weak, don't worry; there is plenty of time to catch up. Below there are a few tips for each category.

Grades

Much of my earlier advice concerning high school applies here, but with slight modification. All medical schools require pre-requisite science classes, usually two years of biology, chemistry and a year of physics. Your pre-med councilors can help you with this. The rest is up to you. A 4.0 grade average (or "straight As") is the goal. Obviously, such an expectation is rarely achievable and needs to be balanced by your other activities, while still allowing time for fun.

I have a few tips to share, of course. As you will note throughout this book, many of the suggestions I make in these early pages will apply to every stage of your career. You will see some repetition, but that's okay because the points are so important that they bear repeating. In addition, you can look at them as you move on to the next steps at a different point on your path. Once you reach this destination, there is no need to go back and re-read this section. However, the points that still apply will be important when you are trying for the next location on your career path.

1) Choosing your major. I personally struggled with science, but found English and political science quite easy, and ultimately chose political science as my major. It is my experience that no major is particularly helpful for admissions. At times, some committee members may favor a "unique" major, but at the end of the day, a minimum overall GPA—usually about a 3.5/4.0—must be met. However you can't have a 4.0 in English and a 3.0 in science. The isolated science GPA is also considered and is usually about a 3.5/4.0 as well. There is no forgiveness below that point. A low GPA is unlikely to even produce an interview. I personally believe that although some gifted individuals have a proclivity for science, it is still hard work for everyone. There are those individuals who do struggle with some humanities. As a student, you should take some courses that are easy for you. One standard question that often arises concerns engineering. This is a personal decision. If you are completely committed to medical school, I would *not* advise this pathway, as it is usually quite rigorous and can negatively impact GPA. However, if you are not sure about medical school, the study of engineering does provide a great "hedge" and still allows for completion of a pre-med curriculum. Engineering is a great field and there are a lot of opportunities for engineers in the medical field. Similarly, if you are still considering another field like law, a political science major or something similar will allow you to follow both pathways at the same time. You may even decide to get two degrees.

2) Build a strong foundation. Challenge yourself, but don't *overchallenge*. This is even more critical than it was in high school. Medical school admission committees are not impressed with As; they expect As. They will scrutinize your schedule and make sure that you are not taking all easy classes, but on the flip side, they will not reward you for taking four engineering classes and getting straight Bs. If you can balance your load by taking two "hard classes" at a time, it is generally easier to excel in all. It is okay to take one or two science classes at a junior college over the summers; indeed, this will probably help

many of you. However taking most or all of your "hard sciences" at junior colleges, while maintaining a light load at your degree granting institution, will raise a "red flag" to admissions committees and possibly hurt your chances. So will taking only one science course at a time. Both a good GPA and a good science GPA are *expected*. Each medical school publishes the average GPA of matriculates. The main lesson is to set your goals high, but don't stress if your results are in the range of accepted applicants.

3) As mentioned earlier, a good exercise is to ask yourself the same questions any admissions officer does as he or she decides which few of several hundred applicants should be interviewed further. What factors would you consider? Would you weigh the GPA and the MCAT the same or differently? A student presenting with a 4.0 GPA and a high MCAT score makes for an easy choice, but since few students achieve that, how would you decide? Keep in mind that while no set formula exists, top tier medical schools grant greater weight to GPAs earned at the higher ranked colleges and universities. You can't do anything about this now, but read ahead and you'll see why I've recommended going to a school with the greatest name recognition. While the school's ranking does not strictly determine admission, it can play a role in decisions concerning borderline candidates.

4) Build on your strong high school foundation. As I mentioned earlier, I wasted time in my first year of college by not studying material I'd covered in high school as if I were seeing it for the first time. Rather than studying seriously, and getting the As so easily within my reach, I worked 30 hours a week at a job. While bartending was fun and I enjoyed the extra money, it didn't help me at all in my medical career. In fact, it weakened my foundation at a time when I needed to strengthen it for medical school. The harder you work at your studies now, the easier they will be later on. Most medical school curricula include courses in genetics, biochemistry and anatomy. If your college offers courses in those areas, take them. Doing well in science classes at this level will help you excel the second time around in medical school.

5) Learn from your mistakes. Remember that an occasional bad grade is okay *if* you use it as an opportunity to reflect on what you could have done differently in the course to master the material. Identify your weaknesses and change the way you study well before the final grade is determined. In my own case, I eventually learned from my mistakes, but not until I became a resident.

6) Ask for help early. Reach out to teachers and TAs for help if you find the material difficult, ideally well before a test. If their advice does not help, seek out others, whether peers or older students, who have a stronger knowledge of the subject. Don't be embarrassed to get help wherever you can find it, and that includes professional tutoring. Tutors' fees are often quite reasonable, sometimes little more than what you would not think twice about spending on a movie. A good tutor can be a good investment. If money is an issue, you can always barter. You may be good at a different subject and be able to tutor your tutor in that as an exchange.

7) Set expectations for yourself and with the test grader on the first day of the class, or even before school starts—up front. A good teacher wants to help you learn, not just get an A. If you fail to get the A you think you deserve on a test or an assignment, go to the teacher. Do not discuss the grade but do ask how you can improve. Remember you are the student. It is your job to figure out what makes your teacher tick. Determine their expectations and exceed them. Arguing with them sometimes works in the short run, but not in the long run when it comes to your reputation, your letters of recommendation and your applications. You may have a strong will and have different opinions. You may even be right. However, the teacher grades you; you do not grade the teacher. When I have disagreed with an instructor, I have usually found in retrospect that the teacher was right. It just took time and maturity for *me* to realize it.

8) Learn to take responsibility for your actions. This is very difficult, but most young adults can begin to make this transition in college. You can only control your actions, no one else's. If you did not get the result that you want, figure out what *you* can do differently. In the end, no one else will be more invested in your progress—than you. So if you don't get the grade or the score you want, don't blame anyone else. Figure out what you can do differently next time, and do it. Learning to use your time constructively is an important skill in medicine and in life.

Standardized Tests

These are the only ways to really compare individuals from different institutions. No matter how hard or easy a college is, the MCAT offers an opportunity for level comparison. Once again, it is really up to you to get the best score that you can get. It is the first of many, many standardized tests that you will take in your career, and quite honestly, it is still not even close to the hardest. While some students are naturally better at taking these tests than others, it's still up to you to figure out how to do your best. However, to prepare for MCAT, I do have a few hints, most of them very similar to the college admissions testing tips.

1) Study like you mean it! I say that a lot because it bears repeating, and it's that important. As mentioned previously, in preparing for standardized college admissions testing, block out time for study and nothing else. No TV, no music, no internet. Testing environments allow no distractions in the test, so avoid them when you study as well. Create an environment similar to that of the test setting every time you study, so you won't freak out when you actually arrive there. Make the most of your study time and you will have more time to spend on other things. Efficiency will matter even more in medical school.

2) You can never start too early. Think about it from this perspective. The Office of Admissions gives about 40% of the value of your application to the MCAT, exactly the same as your GPA. From a logical standpoint, that means that every hour you spend in class, every hour you spend on a study session, every hour you spend writing a paper, should, combined, represent exactly the same amount of time you should spend on the MCAT. In fact, plan on spending even more. While that is probably not possible, it is nonetheless rational considering that the MCAT, as a single test, is even more important than all your grades combined. Don't make the mistake of cramming. The test is too important for last minute study, and should be something you work on over your college career.

3) Take a formal test prep class early on. The test prep classes, like Kaplan have clearly made a difference in scores. There are several and I do not endorse any particular one. However, those students who do not take these classes are clearly at a disadvantage. I personally recommend starting the course in the summer of sophomore year. This gives you enough time to find out where you stand and identifies which subjects are your weakest and need more of your study time. If the materials are beyond your comprehension at first, don't get discouraged. Just keep the books and study them when you start the subjects in school.

4) Study from the review books as a supplement as you learn the material. That way, you will become familiar with the format of the subject for the test. While you should not use it as a primary source, you can certainly

37

do additional questions and problems in real time as they relate to your classes. I would start this practice during your freshman year. If you are taking chemistry, for example, buy a MCAT review book for chemistry as well. Although your primary objective is to study for the class, a close secondary objective is to prepare for the MCAT. This may not be your teacher's objective at all, however. Make sure you cover the material that the MCAT requires in your study while you are learning and have access to TA's and teachers who can help.

5) Study what you don't know, not what you know. It is easy and comforting to study topics you already know well; it feels good to get questions right. It is much harder to study topics you don't know so well, and struggle with. Most practice tests come with a breakdown of subjects and topics covered by each question. Identify your weakest subjects and the questions you always seem to miss, and spend most of your time on those areas. It will take more effort, but staying disciplined and focused will pay off in achieving your highest score.

6) Re-review the materials and take practice tests whenever you can. Obviously, you will be very busy so this will be hard to do. However, the materials will seem manageable if you break them into smaller pieces. Make studying a part of your day. Bring a book along on the train, read while doing laundry or while you are waiting for a class to start. If you go on spring break, study on the plane or get up an hour before your friends. The more you review the materials and the more times you work through the problems, the better prepared you will be. I have taken over 15 of these national tests, ranging from the ACT to cardiothoracic board re-certification exams. Initially, I wasn't a big fan of practice questions. However as the tests became harder, I began to appreciate their value. Because many of the questions are repeated and similar, I would recommend doing as many questions as many times as possible. It is important to understand why the correct answer is correct and the incorrect ones are not, but it is easier to figure out what to study if you already know the question.

7) Remember, the standardized tests don't test what you know, but what everyone should know. This is even more relevant at this point than in high school. You may be years ahead of the subject on the tests and have gotten rusty by now, or forgotten the material. The only way to stay sharp is to practice. Again, this needs to be worked in with your other activities, but if

you only do about 10% more than your peers, you will enjoy tremendous dividends.

8) If you perform below your expectations, you can retake the test. But just as you should not take a test unless you are prepared, don't *retake* it unless you are *fully* prepared. One mistake is bad. Two is a pattern. Einstein defined insanity as doing the same thing over and over and expecting a different result. Choose sanity! Don't do exactly the same preparation for the second time and expect a different outcome. It won't be different. Reflect on what you did well and duplicate it. Reflect on what you did not do well on and change the strategy. There is some evidence to support averaging MCAT scores. Better to take it once, and make sure there is no need to take it twice. Should you need to, however, rerouting, as we'll learn in coming sections, is certainly possible.

Extracurricular activities

Unlike those you might have undertaken in high school, your extra activities now will need to support your decision to enter a career in medicine. They may not be as much fun as previous choices, but they definitely advance you toward your goal.

The most important activity will be shadowing physicians. No MCAT score and no GPA can make up for *not* shadowing. The more you do the better, but whatever choices you pursue must render real experiences that you can cite in support of your decision to enter medicine. One or two shadowing experiences will not be enough. One candidate I encountered stood out for having accumulated experiences with more than 15 physicians. While there is no upper limit to the amount of shadowing you do, be advised that whatever you're able to do must be significant enough to clearly demonstrate that you have invested considerable time and thought in your decision to go into medicine. Record the details of the experience so that you can recall them in an interview and in a personal statement. A word of caution, however. If you have a relative who is a physician, ask him or her to connect you to colleague who is not related. If your parent is a physician, mention it; but do *not* focus on your experience with your mom or dad. Many admissions committees worry that parents may be "forcing" their children into medicine. Although I personally think this borders on insanity (after all, I know my children have a better sense of what the job entails and the sacrifice it requires than someone who shadows a physician a few times—and I cannot *make* my daughters do anything), mine is an unpopular viewpoint. Similarly, don't make the mistake of relying on experiences you or a family member may have had as a patient as your only exposure to medicine. Such family references are lead buoys. It is typical for a patient experience to spark your interest in medicine, and certainly you can discuss the experience; but it is also important to learn about the physician perspective. You need to understand what the doctor does when he leaves the patient's room. You are trying to become a physician, not a patient.

1) Consider adjunct activities, especially if they can lead to paid positions. It can be volunteering at a hospital or nursing home, or performing research in a lab. Whatever your choice, the best option will include some patient contact. I took an Emergency Medical Technician class during the school year and drove an ambulance for a summer; a great experience *and* a great summer job. The whole experience gave me tremendous insight into the field that I was able to communicate later in my interviews and personal statement. That was an outside activity that I did *right*!

2) "Giving back" is never wrong. However, the activity you choose may be regarded as low yield, depending on who is reviewing your application. For example, "Habitat for Humanity" is a great organization that some admission committee members find impressive. I was not one of those individuals. Granted, building homes for the poor clearly demonstrates your desire to give back to society. Great. Step one. Maybe you should help others by building houses. But experience in construction still gives you *no* insight into what it is like to be a physician. Try to combine service with health care. There are plenty of opportunities locally and overseas.

3) If you come from an underrepresented group, participating in an organization unique to your background will be even more important now than it was in high school. Most admission committees, especially in medical school, value diversity. In fact, patients in underserved communities often prefer physicians from similar communities. However, students who may have a similar ethnicity may not have a similar background. For example, if you identify your background as Hispanic but don't speak Spanish, or identify yourself as Native American but don't know what tribe you to which you belong, expect an increased scrutiny over your application. (Some schools will expect you to have a tribal card.) Similarly, while it may be technically true that someone from Egypt can identify as himself as African American, rest assured that such a claim on an application would face close examination and possible rejection. While I am staunchly opposed to this practice, it is the present reality. It is your job to be prepared.

4) Athletics. This is a difficult topic. Many of you will be recruited to various schools to participate in athletics. The experience is terrific! However, sometimes athletics can interfere with studying and affect grades. As soon as this occurs, one must go. If your next step is medical school and your sport is interfering with your school performance, quit the team. Admissions committees fully understand and are impressed by the time commitment that athletics requires, but they don't make any exceptions on the GPA or MCAT cutoff. They won't penalize you however, for recognizing that you can't do both and leaving the team. In fact, they will respect the decision. One of my good friends who eventually made it into medical school played football for four years at a very strong school. He carried a respectable 3.2 GPA and a 32 MCAT. Not good enough! He had to follow the "Rerouting" path that follows and spent another three years after college getting accepted. He was lucky. Often, athletes have to choose a different career. Only participate in athletics if you can achieve the appropriate GPA and MCAT as well as the shadowing experiences.

5) Research. This is a serious consideration, because anyone wanting to achieve a career in medicine should plan on doing research. I will address this topic at length later, but for now, be advised that the metrics of success in research hinge on three factors: the quantity and quality of the research done, the publication of those findings in medical journals, and the amount of money that work may attract in future research grants. The publication process, which is formidable, progresses as follows: hypothesis, study design, protocol submission to Institutional Review Board (IRB), request for change from IRB X1-3, IRB re-submission, IRB approval, data acquisition, data analysis, manuscript preparation, sending to co-authors, revision after co-author review, submission to journal, rejection/request for revision, revision of manuscript, re-submission, eventual acceptance. Your first submission will be an intimidating experience, but once you go through it a few times, your value as a collaborator increases. Unless you have demonstrated that you have participated in the entire process, your value to a researcher will be limited. Ideally, you will have published one to three papers by medical school. A published paper of any authorship, in any journal, on any subject is infinitely more valuable to your application than none at all. And telling your admissions officer, as 95 percent of applicants do, "Well, it was interesting research, but it didn't work out as we planned," translates as no research at all. Building a reliable base of funding sources

that will, ideally, support you through a career, begins early. If you can, volunteer for someone who has already received NIH funding and who has provided opportunities for students to work on grants. A research mentor can also provide the added bonus of a letter of recommendation, wherein he or she can comment on your work ethic and academic potential. This may be particularly useful if your academic record is otherwise less than spectacular. If you are particularly interested and successful, you can apply for a combined MD/PhD degree, offered by most schools.

6) Summers. As previously mentioned, this deserves its own category. Summers should not be squandered. Don't waste them on experiences that do not relate to your medical career. If you are interested in another field, use the summer to explore that career. If you are committed to the health care field, then either do research, shadow physicians, volunteer, get a job in a hospital, take an EMT class, take a couple of moderately challenging science classes at a community college if it will transfer—or any combination of the above. Don't waste it on a slightly higher paying job in a field in which you have no interest. Don't waste it just hanging out, either. If you want to travel, fine, but try to incorporate something useful and clinically relevant if you can. Most importantly, use some of the time to study for the MCAT!

Recommendations

Strong recommendations are expected and the process is usually handled by your school's pre-med office. Some of these offices feel obligated to rank or gauge the candidacy of the student for medical school. This doesn't really help the top students and may hurt others who may be qualified. No rule that I know of says that you have to use their letter. But if you ask for it, you will waive your right to see it. In general, I would only get letters from those teachers and physicians you have shadowed who you think will write a good letter. Just because you can't see a letter of recommendation doesn't mean you can't ask ahead of time. If the response to a query like "Do you feel comfortable writing a strong letter of recommendation for me?" is lukewarm, the letter is also likely to be the same temperature. Ask someone else. It is unlikely that anyone on the admissions committee knows the person writing the letter, but any reservations mentioned in a letter can raise red flags that can potentially hurt your application.

Remember that the strength of your letter is not completely out of your hands; you can help tailor the type of letter you want. Give your letter writers copies of your resume and application essay. You can also provide copies of papers and projects of which you are particularly proud in order to remind your letter writers about the quality of your work. Additionally, you can specify the personal attributes or components of your application that you would like them to highlight. At times, it may be appropriate to offer them a reasonable rough draft. They may not use all the materials that you provide, but they will appreciate your effort. If you make a point to show pride in the details of your application, your letter writers will be more than willing to do the same. Don't forget a thank you note as well as a notification of the final decision, regardless of the outcome. I prefer handwritten communications, but there is no standard.

Personal Statement

It is my opinion that like letters of recommendation, a personal statement can only hurt you. It cannot make up for GPA or MCAT. A solid one is expected. There is no right or perfect way to manage it. There are, however, plenty of ways to mess it up. I can offer a few tips that may help.

1) Start the process as you are investigating a career in medicine. You can write and rewrite it as you go. It is a personal statement that is not just a snapshot in time. If, like a diary, you record some of the unique "ah-ha" experiences as you go along, it will be easier to recall them with details in real time. For example, if you have a great experience shadowing a physician as a freshman, write down some of the details as you begin a personal statement.

2) The subject is you. However, I personally favor insight into why and how you have chosen a medical career. You may be an Olympic athlete, but your description should still relate to how you have decided you are going to medical school. You are applying to medical school, not a coaching position. Explain your desire "to help others" and describe those life experiences that helped you decide that becoming a physician was the way for you to do it. Avoid any overtones of power-seeking behavior.

3) Never discuss money. Any mention it, even though it is a real concern, is another lead buoy. Don't do it. Ever.

4) Avoid discussion of anything controversial. I have seen statements about a stripping career, "coming out of the closet", going to jail and a myriad of other "hot topics." While such experiences may have influenced a decision to enter medicine, it is inappropriate to unload one's intimate personal

details on the statement. It is not therapy. Nothing you disclose should make any reader uncomfortable.

5) Ask other people you trust to read it. Many others. Take or leave their advice, but listen to it.

6) Look at sample statements and those of your friends, especially if they applied a year or two before you and *were* accepted into medical school. Reading letters of those who were rejected can be quite helpful, but not if you do the same thing.

7) As always, pretend you are deciding your own fate. If you were reviewing your own application, what would you expect? That is the best way to decide what to write. Remember, however, that the people making the decisions are not your age. They are probably your parents' age or older. Make sure they understand the references and that their expectations are met, not yours.

Personal Connections

While it may seem early for an undergraduate to worry about connections or networking—it really is *not* too early. Up to this point, your individual performance is responsible for most of your opportunities. Your GPA, MCAT, etc., are what count the most. This will not always be the case. As described earlier, later on, *who* you know will become more important. At the very least, who you know will be a "tie breaker." This will be discussed in much more detail later on. By the time you reach this stage, determining which personal connections can and can't help will become more important.

Connections that help: Any relationship with a prominent individual in a particular field that began in college can help you enter that field. For example, if you think you may want to be a heart surgeon, find a heart surgeon who publishes extensively and ask if, in addition to shadowing, you can start working with him/her now. To find out how to choose a mentor, fast-forward to the section of this book that addresses students already in medical school.

Connections that don't help: Knowing a physician unrelated to the admissions process is of no help. Even knowing someone on the admission committee holds very limited value. This is a very objective process and there is no favoritism. By way of example, I can offer two clear cases. The head of congenital cardiac surgery and the head of cardiology at a highly recognized institution each had a son applying to medical school in the same year. Neither could influence the process. Both young men were reasonable but "on the fence" candidates. Neither was accepted to the medical school at which their parents worked, although the parents did everything they could to help. One physician even left the institution over this issue. Both sons were admitted elsewhere and both had very successful medical careers. Take away: Nothing matters if your MCAT and GPA fall short.

Connections that may help: Any relationship you make. People have long memories. Believe it or not, a few of my college friends and their parents continue to help me to this day. Whether it is supplying good advice, helping me get into business school or donating money in my name, lifelong friends have helped me in part because we have shared so much over the years. Making enemies has *never* helped me, ever. There is no reason to be negative to anyone. It is hard, especially if they are negative towards you. The best advice is just stay away from those individuals. If that is not possible, seek help.

An Alternative Perspective from a Student Entering Medical School

Preparing for med school:

I was well advised on all the requirements—the forms, letters, interviews, references and tests—thanks to Dr. Lee. But the best advice was to start studying early for the MCAT. It should be a part of your daily study a year, or even two years before you take it; don't just cram for it at the end. Dr. Lee's advice on this is great. If you take just 20 or 30 minutes a day to read a section of the MCAT, and then do ten to fifteen questions every single day, you will be well prepared to take that test.

The thing about standardized tests is that a lot of times you know the answer, but they ask the questions in ways that you don't always know. So you have to learn their language, learn how they think and how to answer their questions. And the only way to do that is to do question after question every day. It really does work.

Take every class seriously

For too many, college has become the only place that you don't worry about getting your money's worth. Think about it: how many students are paying high tuitions, and yet don't seem to understand that unless they work, they won't get what they're paying for? They don't go to class, don't read the texts, don't do the assignments—and yet they're paying for what all those things supposedly render: knowledge, skills and a degree that means something. Success in school requires an attitude toward learning and I don't think it can be taught in the school itself. Attitudes and expectations definitely figure in the trajectory that is the process of getting into medical school and moving through the training.

The importance of mentors

I cannot emphasize enough the value of mentors, and encourage students to actively seek them out. I've had some great ones just through my experience thus far and great relationships with every professor who wrote a letter of recommendation for me.

I'd say to students, reach out to people—professors, doctors, anyone—whose work interests you. Say "I'm really interested in what you're doing," and ask if you can learn more, maybe work with them in some way.

The importance of research

Most research on campuses is carried out by undergrads. When I was an undergrad, I made a point of going around and talking to six or seven professors. If a paper of theirs interested me, I sought them out and told them I was interested in talking to them and learning more. One professor I approached assigned me to a project with three graduate students. He told us this was our project and to be as innovative as we wanted. It was a great experience because we did all kinds of things and ended working on two papers together. I worked for this professor for three years and we've kept in touch long afterward. By now he's seen me through a lot of different things in my life, and that's just invaluable to me personally as well as professionally.

The value of networking

Networking is *huge*. In fact, a lot of medical education is about making human connections.

A professor in my MPH program had worked for the CDC for 25 years. He was also the CEO of Doctors of the World, a renowned NGO, and very well connected with the whole global disaster aid world. I ran into him not long ago and when I told him I was going to Columbia, where he'd taught for a time, he got very excited, insisting "I've got two people you have to meet!" I met him two days ago and he wanted me to meet someone *else,* who was the head epidemiologist for Human Rights Watch. As I'm totally on a human rights kick, this is really exciting for me.

Another time I asked a professor whose lecture I found interesting how to get an internship with the organization he discussed. He said, "You want the internship? I'll get it for you." And picked up his phone right there!

It really is a matter of approaching professors and any other professionals. Be sincerely interested in them and their work, and they will be willing to talk to you, and help you too. It's amazing to me how much you can accomplish this way, how much you can learn and grow.

The importance of publishing early

Publishing is very good, and if you can do it before applying to medical school it's *really* good. I've already published some; in fact I'm working on something now. But it's also hard to do when you're an undergrad because you don't know a great deal about the process, which is long and tedious. I took one technical writing course that was very good, but apart from that, even if you're lucky enough to take such a class, you just don't have much direction. All the more reason to network, find people who can show you how.

AN ALTERNATIVE PERSPECTIVE FROM A CARDIOLOGY FELLOW

Publishing as a key step on your career path

Publishing may be more important now than ever before. In fact, I think it's increasingly important to publish before you even apply to medical school.

Students planning on medical school can always get some research work in a dog lab, which a lot of kids do. But I'd encourage prospective applicants to go around to a lot of different labs and see which ones they like. A good avenue to explore is clinical studies, which I tried and liked a lot. I found a great power house group working in outcome clinical studies, which was great for me because I learned a lot from their thought processes that enabled me to publish early and easily.

My research mentor gave me some very good advice early on. He said, "When you talk about your research in an interview, whoever you're talking to is going to be able to tell whether you care about it or not. You may know a lot about some random ion channel in the heart of a dog, but if you don't care about it much that will come through. However if you've got one study you're excited about, that will impress more than having three or four random studies in which you're just going through the motions."

Get Directions: Medical School Admission

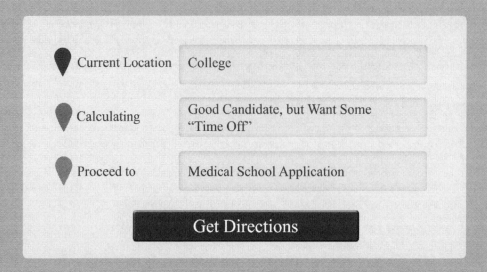

Current Location — College

Calculating — Good Candidate, but Want Some "Time Off"

Proceed to — Medical School Application

Get Directions

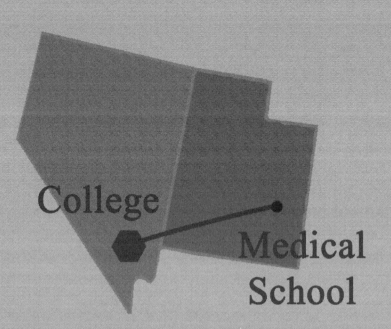

College

Medical School

Taking a Year Off

For those of you who, nearing completion and are confident that you will get into medical school, want to take a break between college and medical school—don't! You are barely beginning a long journey. It is an enjoyable and rewarding one, but it will certainly be more challenging than college was. If you feel you need a break now, maybe you should choose a different path. If you want to try something different because you are young, I would encourage you to embark on a semester or year abroad, take a light course load and explore. This is still a bit of a red flag to admissions officers, but an experience relevant to medicine may prove an advantage. For example, it is easy to explain that spending one year studying Spanish in Spain and traveling around Europe will help you learn the language so you can communicate with your non-English speaking patients in the future. Taking a year off to work as a ski instructor is not so easy to explain, and it will certainly not impress. It is better to complete your college in five years to show that you carried a heavy science load before and/or after your year abroad. I would recommend doing it between years two and three, as later it will interfere more with the application process. Ideally, if you do this, you should also try to relate it to medicine. Make sure you work with your school to stay enrolled the entire time. However, I would recommend that you do not take time off, as this is the safest path. Put yourself in the shoes of the admission committee members. Who would you rather admit: someone who needed time off or someone who demonstrated unwavering commitment for four years or longer? There are plenty of those "perfect" students competing for the same spot.

A word of caution. If you choose to ignore this advice, or you really need to take one or two years off, I would recommend staying connected with the health care field and taking some classes to remain engaged with school. Taking too much time off without demonstrating continued commitment to healthcare and an ability to perform in an academic environment is likely to raise potentially irreversible concerns with the admission committee, which may require additional formal study prior to acceptance (or non-acceptance). You may have to choose a different career.

An alternate pathway is to gain acceptance into medical school and then apply for a deferral. You have to have a good reason to warrant one, but a deferral allows you to keep your acceptance and start a year later. I personally started on this pathway, applying for and receiving a deferral that would allow me to spend a year in Spain to learn Spanish. Fortunately my parents intervened and convinced me to go right to medical school. Nonetheless, this is a much better option than applying after a year off. If you are denied a deferral, you can still get time away for these activities during medical school if you need it.

AN ALTERNATIVE PERSPECTIVE FROM A STUDENT ENTERING MEDICAL SCHOOL

The value of exploring options

I think it's very important to understand the long term trajectory through medical school and beyond. It *is* a series of steps, and each one is critical to development. But I also think there is considerable value in stepping off the path at times to broaden your experience, which is one reason I opted to do a master's in public health. I was on a five-year track for my bachelor's, but then I realized that by taking one or two classes in the summer, I could finish in four.

So what could I do in that year? I started looking around and considered just working in a lab, or maybe getting a "real job." But then I discovered public health, which interested me a lot, and when I realized doing MPH would fit in with my plans, the decision was easy. By that time I realized that I didn't have to be a private practice physician; that I could be a public health physician, something completely different from what I'd always thought about medicine.

What I like about public health is its preventative approach, drawn from a holistic understanding of the context—the conditions, education, lifestyle, culture—of people's lives. Medicine focuses on treatment, which is important of course, but I'm learning that we also need to understand more than just treatment. Let's treat this person but let's make sure his conditions at home are such that he doesn't have to come back to us.

The value of gaining a broad range of medical experiences

When I arrived at George Washington University to start my MPH last June, I immediately set about exploring options and making connections. I worked my way into the International HIV/AIDS Conference, made some contacts, and then got an internship with the United Nations' World Food Program where I worked for four months. Then I worked in a STD Clinic in a low income South Washington D.C. neighborhood, where I implemented mental health and substance abuse screening programs and saw things I'd never encountered before. Then I volunteered in a gay men's clinic, where I did interviewing and counseling, and gained more new insights.

Taking a year out at some point to engage in different medical learning experiences is one of the best things you can do. What you *don't* want to do is just travel around somewhere without building in a serious learning experience in medicine. You can't explain away a year of just travel.

AN ALTERNATIVE PERSPECTIVE FROM A CHAIRMAN OF INTERNAL MEDICINE

On not following a structured path

I think there is a lot to be said for allowing for a certain amount of serendipity as you move along your career path. Of course many students who follow a more traditional, structured path achieve good careers. Quite often their parents are doctors or professors. Quite often they go to a highly ranked college, then a highly ranked medical school, and then they get into an outstanding residency program. Everything flows in an ordered sequence and they do well. But I've also known some to follow that path and end up dysfunctional, even though everything has gone according to plan.

On the value of allowing for random opportunities

I've been struck by the degree to which many of my career choices were essentially accidents. For example, I can remember being a medical student and saying to people, "I don't know what I'm going to do, except maybe just an assistant professor somewhere. Whatever I end up doing though, is going to have *nothing* to do with a microscope."

But I ended up having a strong research career that involves a great many microscopes and other laboratory equipment, largely through a series of unintended diversions. For example, I fell under the influence of a very strong and internationally famous professor of liver disease in South Africa, whose teaching was very clear, very structured and organized. It fit very well with my way of thinking and I worked with him for some time.

Then after serving my tour in the South African army, I went into internal medicine without really thinking about it. Normally the progression in my field is internal medicine followed by gastroenterology, and then hepatology. However in my case, I never went through gastroenterology, again due to an unintended detour. My hepatology professor had connections with the NIH. I might have gone into a program that was very different, very clinical, but through the NIH, which invited me to come to the US, I ended up in a very strong research environment that turned out to be perfect for me.

So I would caution against trying to structure things too much, because if you're able to be a little more open to opportunities, surprising things can happen.

Get Directions: Medical School Admission

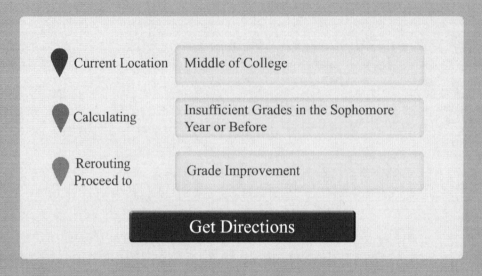

Current Location — Middle of College

Calculating — Insufficient Grades in the Sophomore Year or Before

Rerouting Proceed to — Grade Improvement

Get Directions

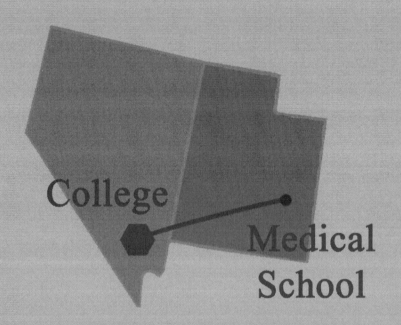

College

Medical School

Insufficient Grades Before Junior Year

This was the category I was in. I'd seen most of the material in high school and spent time working outside of school. I didn't mind taking quizzes without being fully prepared—a practice that did not produce many "A's". About halfway through college, my GPA was low; *way* too low. It was clear that I wasn't going to be a competitive candidate for medical school. My pre-med advisor told me not to apply to Medical School but plan on going to a "post-bac" program (discussed later). I realized that to achieve an acceptable GPA, I would need to improve my grades by at least 50 percent or more. Usually, application to medical school occurs in the beginning of your senior year, so you really only have the first three years' worth of grades at the time you submit your application.

I decided to take a year off in order to use all the grades from my senior year. In my case, I knew that even a good junior year would not compensate for two mediocre years, and that I would need two years of hard work to improve my chances for acceptance. I cut back the hours of my part-time job. I took several somewhat redundant science classes to increase my science GPA. I also stacked my schedule with five or six classes at a time, instead of the typical four, so that I could increase my overall GPA. It worked. I didn't get a 4.0 but I did make the dean's list during those years. Although my GPA was not great overall, it met the minimum requirements for acceptance at the mid-tier schools. I spent the next year working as a sleep study technician, applying for medical school and taking Spanish classes. Since I was actually working in a hospital, it was viewed as a good use of time to gain experience in healthcare. When I was eventually accepted, I took the summer off and went to Spain. My plan, while somewhat unorthodox, worked for me but I was lucky. Looking back now, I realize that it really would have been much easier if I had just worked a little harder the first two years. It took me a couple of detours to learn this lesson, but I'm glad I did. I hope by reading this, you can learn from my mistakes.

The important thing to understand is that a mediocre GPA in the first or second year can still be turned around with a lot of hard work and dedication. Your studies must take precedence over everything else. If activities like athletics, a part-time job or volunteering take time away from schoolwork, drop them. No other activity, no matter how worthy, can make up for a low GPA—not even a perfect MCAT.

Get Directions: Medical School Admission

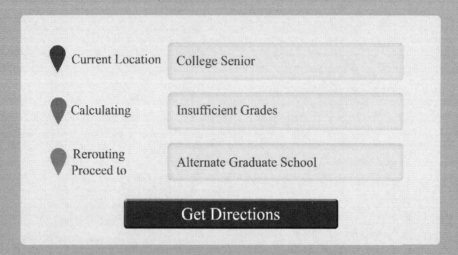

Current Location	College Senior
Calculating	Insufficient Grades
Rerouting Proceed to	Alternate Graduate School

Get Directions

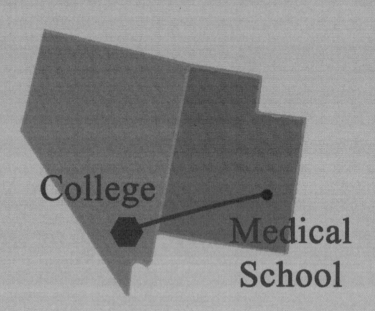

College

Medical
School

Insufficient Grades Senior Year

If your grades are clearly too low and you are unlikely to get in, I would not apply yet. I think there is a stigma against people who apply and fail. Most admissions committees track candidates who have applied previously to their school. If you are "on the cusp," applying makes sense. If acceptance seems a stretch because your grades are too low for any medical school (MD or DO), then apply to an alternate graduate school instead. If you are truly "on the cusp," I would recommend pursuing both paths simultaneously. That way if you are not accepted into medical school, you won't waste an additional year waiting for the next school admission cycle without an active plan in place.

Several programs offer formalized post-baccalaureate pre-med curriculum, often termed "post-bac" programs. They are essentially pre-med courses for late decision makers who did not take the required science classes in college. However, there are also several post-graduate programs that are essentially "second chances" for slow starters. Often such a program, taken side by side with medical students, is a light version of the first year of medical school that can lead to a master's degree. Demonstrating success in a program like this gives you a chance for admission. The critical thing is to realize that the odds are against you and that you need to identify which programs have successful track records for placement into medical school. They are usually quite expensive, so if you are going to commit the time and expense, make sure that you are successful.

Other degrees have value and also can accomplish the same end. For example, an advanced degree in pharmacology or anatomy is likely to help later in medical school. A master of public health degree can also be useful later in your career. If you are never accepted into medical school, such degrees give you another career option. There are many of these types of degrees, but I would only recommend doing one in science. Also, realize that going this route won't be necessarily prove one's potential for medical school, and may not prove as strong a choice as the "second chance" pathway. However, another career option is worth considering at this point. It is a personal decision that you need to make for yourself. I would personally have chosen a degree that gives me another career option. In retrospect, I would have probably obtained my MPH in my "year off."

A word of caution. Recognize that no matter what degree you sign up for, *every* medical school will expect its completion prior to matriculation. Dropping out after you achieve acceptance is not an option. Therefore, if you choose a PhD or any advanced degree, make sure you can complete it before medical school begins.

Get Directions: Medical School Admission

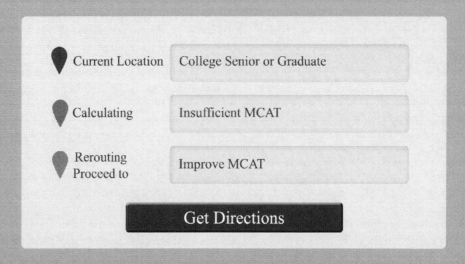

Current Location	College Senior or Graduate
Calculating	Insufficient MCAT
Rerouting **Proceed to**	Improve MCAT

Get Directions

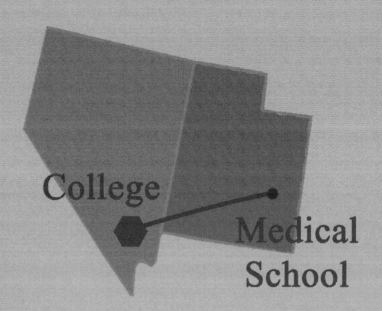

College

Medical
School

Insufficient MCAT

The importance of the MCAT (Medical College Admissions Test) cannot be overemphasized. While there are cut-offs for interview and acceptance, in most institutions the results of MCAT determine about 40% of the weight of an application. Although this may seem "unfair," the test represents the only way to measure candidates head to head. It is very difficult to assess the difficulty of a curriculum, even in a "top tier" school. Everyone takes the same MCAT.

I have heard many excuses for a poor MCAT during interviews, but even the good ones are pretty lame. At the end of the day, even if you are a poor standardized test taker, then it is up to you to get better. The MCAT is only the first medical standardized test you will take, and it is *not* the hardest. There will be USMLE Step 1, USMLE Step 2, USMLE Step 3, USMLE Step 2 CS, and specialty boards. If you can't figure out the MCAT, perhaps medical school is not for you.

The good news is that many students have retaken the MCAT and improved their scores enough to get into medical school. There is no perfect or single strategy, but I can offer a few suggestions.

1) Change the way you prepared for the last one. Albert Einstein is credited with defining insanity as doing the same thing over and expecting different results. Don't do the same thing over.

2) Get help! Nothing beats studying, but what you study matters. If you haven't taken a prep class, do so. They have tremendous data bases of questions. Do them all; do them often. If you have taken one, consider taking a different one. It may be better for you.

3) Concentrate on your greatest weakness. One of my strengths has always been reading and I often take it for granted. Some of my colleagues have struggled with this section. They have advised taking a speed reading class. I am not sure if it helps, but clearly focusing on your weakness should be the main focus.

4) Maintain your strengths. Don't slip on the scores that were good. It is actually easier to improve a point or two on your strong sections than to improve a lot in one.

5) Make sure you are going to do significantly better. If not, don't retake it. Apply with what you have. The practice tests are not perfect, but they are a good gauge of how well you might do. If you are not capable of a satisfactory score, it would be wise to consider another option, another related career in medicine.

Get Directions: Medical School Admission

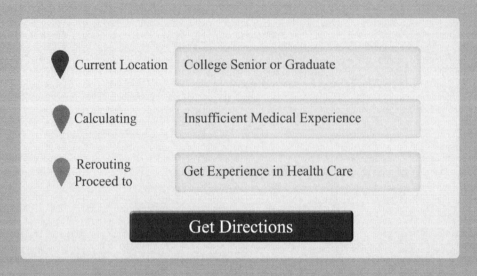

Current Location	College Senior or Graduate
Calculating	Insufficient Medical Experience
Rerouting Proceed to	Get Experience in Health Care

Get Directions

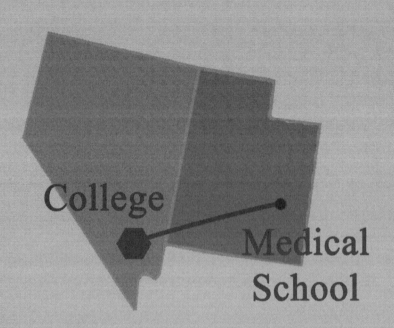

College

Medical School

Insufficient Medical Experience

One of my friends had a 3.5 from the University of Pennsylvania, where he played football for four years. He had a good MCAT, but he did not get into medical school at first. He spent two years doing research in a cardiovascular lab, but ultimately was not accepted and chose a different pathway.

At the time I couldn't figure out why, even though I was already a resident and had graduated from medical school. After my experience on the admissions committee as an attending physician, the reason became clear. He never got involved in patient care. If I could turn back time and give him good advice at that moment in his life, he would be a physician now.

There is a son of a famous physician couple; the mother was a plastic surgeon, the father a cardiothoracic surgeon. His sister was a resident in neurosurgery. He had decent grades, a low but a decent MCAT and two years of research. Nonetheless, he was twice rejected from medical school. Why? His only experience in medicine was via his family. After shadowing non-family members, he was ultimately accepted. Unfortunately, even his brilliant, successful family members did not know *how* the process worked. They only knew some of the things that they had done right.

Admissions committees are comprised of PhDs, MDs and people of all different backgrounds who have many different perspectives. However, they share two characteristics in common: they are bright and they can recognize insincerity immediately. If you don't investigate the field from the perspective of non-relative physicians, you will not get in. If you wait until you are applying to recognize and address this reality, you can expect a poor result at the end of the process.

If you are reading this book as a college junior or senior and realize that you don't have the required experience, make it your number one priority to get it. If you are reading this book after you have unsuccessfully applied and a lack of actual patient care experience is clearly a weakness, take a year to work in a hospital, work as a clinical trials research assistant, draw blood, and otherwise shadow as much as possible. While a lack of patient contact represents a deficit in your application, a little effort on your part can lead to the kind of work that will turn this around. Make sure, however that when the committee asks "What is different about this application from last time?" that the answer will be apparent and substantial.

Get Directions: Medical School Admission

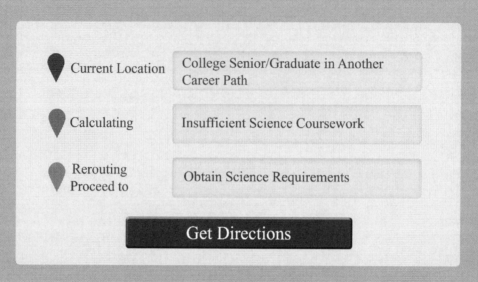

Current Location — College Senior/Graduate in Another Career Path

Calculating — Insufficient Science Coursework

Rerouting Proceed to — Obtain Science Requirements

Get Directions

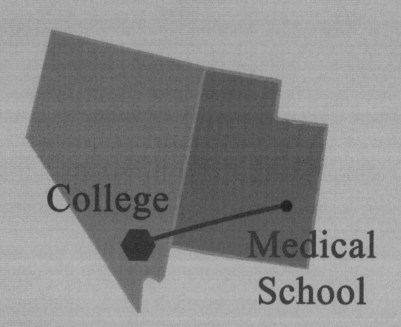

College

Medical School

Insufficient Science Coursework

So you've decided you really do want to pursue a career in medicine but don't have the required classes. No problem! Remember you are not alone; many others have gone before you. There are many pathways to return to the main path. You can reach out to your pre-med advisor. If you have not yet graduated, you may be able to delay graduation and extend college. If you have graduated, you may want to consider several excellent formal programs, both full and part time, that are essentially concentrated pre-med courses for late decision makers. Just remember that all the other criteria for acceptance to medical school outlined in the previous chapters—the MCAT, shadowing, recommendations and personal statement—remain fixed.

My cousin Nick was typical of many students unsure of their path. At the end of his junior year, he decided that he did not want to be an engineer. He contacted me, shadowed me and multiple other physicians and decided that he wanted to be a physician. He spent the next two years completing his pre-med requirements and studying for the MCAT and applied. He clearly was going to have a "gap year" so he enrolled in a master of public health program and volunteered in a men's health center. By the time he applied, he had all the requirements, plus a great track record and a "story" that made sense. He was readily accepted to Columbia School of Medicine. However, had he neglected to shadow extensively, had he done poorly on his science coursework and the MCAT; had he squandered the "gap year" or failed to demonstrate an active commitment to medicine before and after the decision—he would still be working in the "Rerouting" section instead of advancing to the next step.

Get Directions: Choosing Medical School

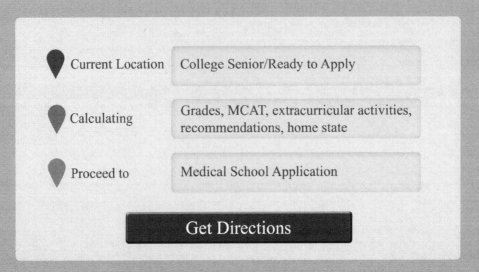

Current Location	College Senior/Ready to Apply
Calculating	Grades, MCAT, extracurricular activities, recommendations, home state
Proceed to	Medical School Application

Get Directions

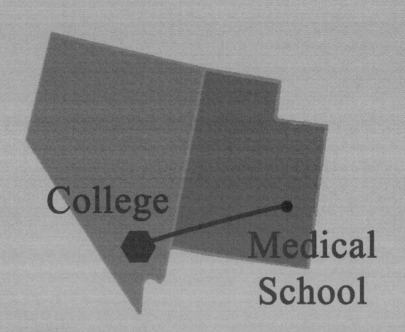

College

Medical School

Medical School Application Tips

There are approximately 140 MD awarding institutions and 30 DO awarding institutions in the United States. Generally, there are two types of schools; those that prefer or exclusively accept in-state residents and those that have no preference. Most of the information concerning admissions data is public, but the majority of medical students attend schools in states where they attended high school, not necessarily college. The choice of where to apply is a highly personal decision, but only partially under your control. I have a few tips for this step.

1) About a third of your applications should be submitted to schools with the highest ranking for which you think you are a reasonable candidate, even if these are schools that may be a reach for you. Generally, reputations of medical school reputations are ranked in the same way as undergraduate schools, and are likewise available in the US News and World Report's annual rankings. Admission to a top 10 or top 15 schools is useful, but be sensitive to cost. (See below.) Reputation is important, but not critical at this stage.

2) Another third of your applications should be submitted to schools for which you are solid candidate (accepting candidates with similar mean GPA and MCAT scores). If you have a 30 MCAT and the school average is a 35, unless you are a unique candidate, admission is improbable and your focus may be better served elsewhere.

3) The last third of your applications should be submitted to schools for which you consider yourself an exceptionally good candidate (higher than mean GPA and MCAT). *No one* is guaranteed a spot. Medical school is competitive. Every admission is valuable. No matter where you are accepted, you can achieve a very successful career only if you are accepted.

4) The only disincentive to apply to EVERY school is economic, so use your personal situation to decide how many schools are reasonable. I would personally apply to as many reasonable schools as I could afford. Most admissions officers now recommend applying to at least ten or twelve.

5) MD vs. DO. I favor the MD. The DO route is great and, like everything else, offers some advantages. In particular, it uniquely offers osteopathic manipulative medicine, a type of manual therapy. In general, admission requirements may be softer for DO schools (average MCAT 27 vs. 31, average GPA 3.5 vs. 3.7), but they are also very competitive and many students are candidates for both. A 2010 survey of students applying to both MD and DO schools in the United States found that 35% were admitted only to a DO school, 11% were admitted only to an MD school, and 26% were admitted to both. The remaining 52% were not admitted to any schools. Both disciplines/programs are recognized equally by state and federal regulations. As of July 2015, the American Osteopathic Association, American Association of Colleges of Osteopathic Medicine and the Accreditation Council for Graduate Medical Education will create a single, unified accreditation system for graduate medical education programs in the United States. However, I personally believe that DO schools offer less access to some specialty fields in post-graduate training, like cardiac surgery. The math is simple: 20,000 students each year go into MD schools, and 6,000 go into DO schools. Since some of the fields are dominated by MDs, there may be some bias in favor of MDs when selecting trainees. Whether this is true or not is unclear, but at this point, you probably don't know what field you will end up in, so it makes sense to me to keep all options open. An MD is a bit safer and also allows for greater recognition abroad.

6) International vs. US medical schools. I think it is advantageous to attend a mainland medical school if possible, but if you only get into one school and it happens to be international, take it. You can't move on without a degree. You can get anywhere once that occurs and there are several effective ways to be successful no matter where you obtain your MD.

7) Consider where you want to end up. Although movement is frequent, there seems to be an increasing gravitation over time to remain at your last geographic location. If you want to end up in a highly competitive state like California, it is best to work on a plan in parallel with that goal.

8) Consider visiting schools before you apply. If you are on vacation in a city with a medical school at any time during college, try to take a couple of hours one day to tour the school. If you go to Mardi Gras or the Kentucky Derby, get up an hour or two before your friends one day and check out a school. Whether you like it or hate it, a tour will be worth your time.

9) Consider cost. According to the American Association of Medical Colleges (AAMC), the median four year cost of attendance for the class of 2014 attending an in-state college or university is $218,898 for a public school and $286,806 for a private school. The median debt a medical student carries is roughly $170,000 for public schools and $190,000 for private school graduates. Median! If you choose a long residency and need to defer repayment as I did, this amount may double before you can start paying back. Roughly, that could mean $400,000. If you pay it back over 20 years, expect payments of $20,000 per year. Since your disposable income will come after you pay taxes, you would effectively be spending $30,000 of your pre-tax income on debt. For example, even an income of $150,000 a year drops to $120,000 immediately. Don't let this discourage you, but do try to keep the debt as low as possible. There are options to explore, like committing to work for the military or for an underprivileged population. These are all good options, but will limit your practice location and likely limit your specialty. I personally preferred to pay the money and keep my options open, but I did research during medical school and received a state scholarship to keep costs down. I also chose to go to the University of Illinois, where tuition at the time was substantially lower. Do not let cost be the only factor, but do make it factor.

Get Directions: Choosing Medical School

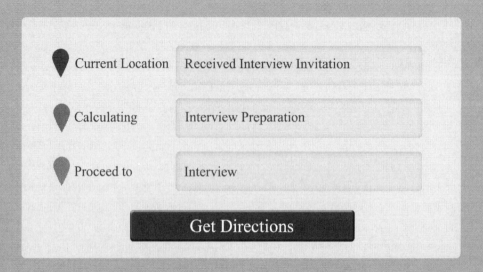

Current Location   Received Interview Invitation

Calculating   Interview Preparation

Proceed to   Interview

Get Directions

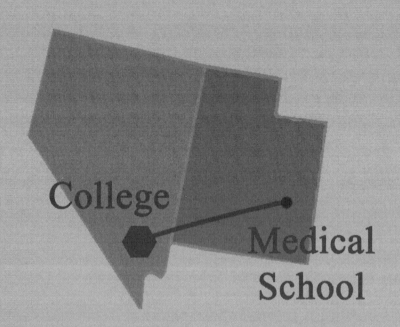

College

Medical
School

Interview Preparation

If you have an interview, you have a shot. While the other components of admission are still critical, the interview can actually help you, hurt you or do nothing at all for your application. Since you obviously want it to help, here are a few tips to ensure that it goes well.

1) Be prepared. Research the school. Study what they place on the website. Ask to talk to students there before the interview to learn what you can about the interviewing doctor. Google him or her. However, candidates should be careful to not bring up too much. You don't want to come across as a stalker. If he or she went to the same school as your mom or dad, a simple query ("Where did you go to school?") may open up a nice connection even if you already know the answer. A group interview, should the school utilize one, will not be a secret so you should not be surprised.

2) Be positive. Points are never awarded for cynicism or negativity. This is something that is hard work and requires constant recalibration for someone like myself. Just think about who you would rather be around. It is usually positive people.

3) Be honest. Never lie.

4) Be confident. Don't make excuses or blame for a poor performance. The best answer I ever got was to a question I asked a young man about his MCAT score, which was a 29. I asked if he thought about retaking the test. "I did, but I didn't score a lot higher on the practice test," he said. "I am actually quite proud of that score. I studied hard and that is the best I could do. I would have liked to do better but I prepared as best as I could. I think my GPA and course load reflect my ability to compete in the classroom." Now

an MCAT of 29 still is not as good as the 35 scored by another applicant, but it's a lot better than the 30 scored by the student who complained that there was an alarm going off in the background, or any one of a thousand other excuses students can generate.

5) Practice makes perfect, so rehearse your responses. Only a handful of questions are asked routinely. "Why do you want to go to medical school? What are your strengths? What are your weaknesses? Did you ever have a conflict? What was it and how did you manage it?" Write down your answers and practice them. Don't memorize answers, but do create a framework of a few key points that you would like to make. Try to practice interview with someone who has taken part in the admissions process. Most importantly, LISTEN to their feedback and advice.

6) Look the part. You are interviewing for a spot in medical school; not going out with your friends. Choose an image of a physician that your mom or dad would go to see. Use that as your target "look."

7) Never talk about money.

8) Never talk about power.

AN ALTERNATIVE PERSPECTIVE FROM
A STUDENT ENTERING MEDICAL SCHOOL

The value of well-rounded background, academically and personally

From what I'm seeing among med school applicants now, is that most people really interested in medicine are really more interested in "helping" anyway, in whatever capacity. For example of the 25 applicants I talked to while interviewing at Columbia University School of Medicine, only one of them was coming directly to medical school as an undergrad. I met one young woman who had been an opera singer for four years. She had grown up in the Bronx, trained in Texas, and then returned to New York. She was performing in different venues around the city when she realized she wanted something else. So she did an accelerated pre-med science credit program at NYU, and applied to Columbia. Columbia, I notice, seems keen to admit people of atypical backgrounds because they perceive, correctly, I think, that they bring something valuable to the profession.

In fact, I'm hearing that medical schools are now seeking applicants who present with well-rounded personal and academic backgrounds, perhaps because they feel that they will be better able to connect with people. If I'm a brilliant 4.0 science major but I have no people skills, then I may be great in the clinical sense but patients are not going to *like* me.

So it's very important to develop interests beyond medicine, especially in the liberal arts. Columbia is actually at the epicenter of what they call "narrative medicine," the theory that medical practice should be comprised of competence complemented by understanding of the complex narratives linking doctors, colleagues, patients and the public. This was started some years ago by a woman MD at Columbia who took time off to earn a PhD in English, and then came back to push for changes in medical education. Columbia now offers a master's degree in narrative medicine, wherein you take a lot of classes in literature, humanities, art, history and philosophy. The master's integrates into your normal program.

Get Directions: Obtaining a Residency

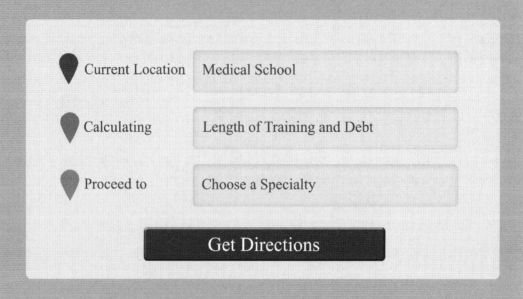

Current Location — Medical School

Calculating — Length of Training and Debt

Proceed to — Choose a Specialty

Get Directions

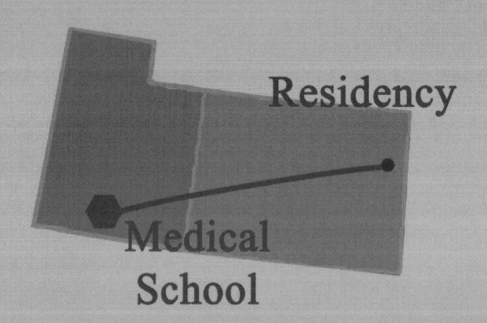

Residency

Medical School

Looking Towards Residency

"I am in a good medical school. What next?"

Medical school curricula are evolving, but in general, the first two years are comprised primarily of basic science courses offering very little clinical exposure. At the end of the second year, all students take the United States Medical Licensing Exam Step 1. After the student passes that, he or she begins clinical rotations with mostly "hands on" experience in the hospital and clinics. In the beginning of year four, the student applies to residency. No matter which residency the student chooses, the same five components determine competitiveness of application: grades, USMLE score, research, recommendations and medical school reputation. I'll discuss each of these at length in the following chapters, as well as how to decide which path to take and how to choose an academic versus a private practice pathway.

Recognize that residency is really extended training. The length of a residency varies from three to over ten years. It seems like a long time, but actually, when you consider that you will likely be practicing for up to 40 years, an extra few years do not seem like much.

Also recognize that your income will be limited during residency. According to the AAMC, the median 1st post-MD Year salary is $50,214. It doesn't go up much until you finish training. The median 4th post-MD Year is $56,380, which is usually enough to live frugally. If possible, I would encourage as much loan repayment as you can manage at this time. At the very least, get rid of credit card debt. Of course circumstances may dictate otherwise. In our case, with two kids and my wife in medical school, all we could afford was to let the interest and debt accrue. In addition, we accumulated more than $70,000 on our credit cards. We had to live frugally, much as we did while residents, for more than 10 years after the end of training. Looking back, what we received in satisfaction clearly made those lean years a bargain.

I would not make any choice in residency on the basis of income or debt. The only thing I would encourage is to minimize the amount of debt you accrue during medical school and beyond. At this point, reputation of residency is increasingly important and the cost differential increasingly inconsequential. After completion of residency, the candidates from the "top institutions" will be qualified for more positions and measurably larger first salaries.

AN ALTERNATIVE PERSPECTIVE FROM A STUDENT ENTERING MEDICAL SCHOOL

On choosing a specialty

I've not gotten to that point yet, but I do think lifestyle and the personalities of the doctors you meet in the field are major determining factors. Certainly the kind of life the field will offer in terms of personal and family time is very important to most of us now. That may be why I'm noticing new trends in choices of specialties. For example, you see more people going into dermatology or ENT, and while some of those programs are competitive, they may be competitive not because you have to be a brilliant doctor, but because the lifestyle is considered good. You'll make a good income and you'll have regular shifts.

But then doing what you're passionate about plays a major role too, so it's good to try things early on. If you do a surgery rotation and then find out you hate the people and hate the work, well, you've learned something important about yourself as well as the field.

I think that no matter what you choose, it comes down to how you set your priorities. You can say: "I want this residency but my family is still my priority. So I will give my all to my residency when I'm there, but when I'm home, my family is all. I'm not going to happy hour or a game with the guys. My family comes first."

AN ALTERNATIVE PERSPECTIVE FROM A DEPARTMENT CHAIR OF INTERNAL MEDICINE

On choosing a specialty

There are many wrong reasons to make a career choice. Choosing something because a spouse has won a spot somewhere—"Oh I'll just go and do whatever's available"—is a bad choice, though sometimes you have to make it. Another negative choice is deciding you're not smart enough to do what you really want, so you do something less challenging. It's very important to choose something you can really enjoy and be passionate about. I consider myself very lucky at this stage of my career, which admittedly is advanced, to be able to come to work every day and do things I love.

AN ALTERNATIVE PERSPECTIVE FROM A FEMALE ASSISTANT PROFESSOR

The challenges and rewards of a medical career for women

I think it's true that women face certain choices in attempting to combine family and career that men don't. In my own case, I'd originally planned on a career in surgery, but later changed to radiology and mammography. Granted, this field is more accommodating to family life than surgery is, but I know I would have made that decision even if I hadn't married and had children. I love radiology, but then the field doesn't draw as many women as men. I was one of three women in a residency class of 20. For the most part, I never let my personal life interfere with my work, but that's not always possible for men or women, something else you need to accept.

As for schools being supportive of women students and residents, I don't think my medical school was as supportive as my residency was. For example, I had my first baby on a Monday and my medical school *required* that I take a final exam the following Friday—so I came in to take it with my four-day-old baby.

We've been talking about the negatives, but the positives of a medical career are just *immense*. The two best things that ever happened to me are becoming a physician and having children. Yes, women face some extra choices along the way, like when to plan your family, how to manage your support systems and even what specialty will ultimately offer the best fit. But once you get past residency and into practice, things are rewarding beyond anything you can imagine. Now when I'm at work, I *love* what I do; I'm energized and fully engaged. There is none of what sometimes seemed like drudgery during those residency years. Our children, now 13 and 15, are doing well. This is a very fulfilling time.

Get Directions: Obtaining a Residency

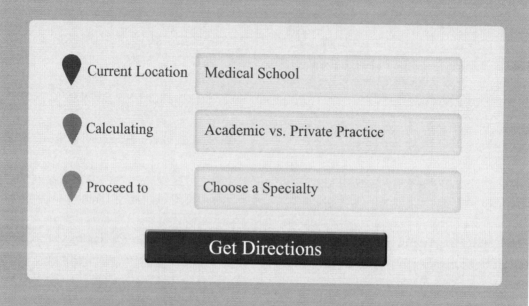

▼	Current Location	Medical School
▼	Calculating	Academic vs. Private Practice
▼	Proceed to	Choose a Specialty

Get Directions

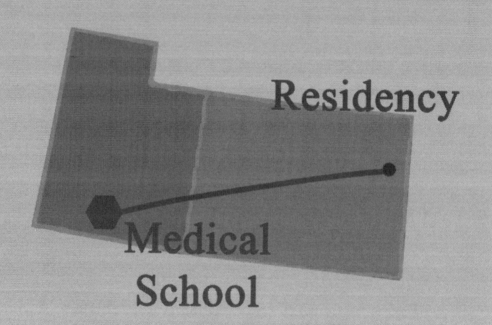

Residency

Medical School

Academic vs. Private Practice

There are two major choices you will need to make in the next three years: one is between an academic and a private practice, and the other is which field you will enter.

One is easy, one is hard. I think the decision to go down the academic path is easy and will discuss in detail below. Like everything else, although you can start one route and change you mind later, it is much easier if you start on the academic pathway initially and change to private than if you start on the private pathway and decide to do academics.

Academic versus private practice. Both academic and private practice physicians take care of patients and achieve great personal satisfaction. While both can and do engage in research, research is usually essential for the promotion of academic physicians. Similarly, while both can train residents and medical students, teaching is part of the academic surgeon's job description. In general, all academic physicians are involved in research and education; the majority of private practice physicians are not.

In the end, the choice between a private and an academic practice is a personal one, depending on the individual. However, I feel the best choice at this critical point—the beginning of your medical education—is the academic one. I can come up with a myriad of reasons to support why I believe you should start on the academic pathway and attempt to outline them below. While all are philosophical, most are pragmatic.

1) In addition to providing state-of-the-art care to the sickest patients, academic physicians receive the added privilege and responsibility of discovering new knowledge, transmitting it to others and mentoring the next generation.

2) It is easier to transition from academics to private practice. It is difficult to go the other way around. The first rule of life is: "There are exceptions to

85

every rule." However, you should be aware of trends. The path to a career in academic medicine is a long one. Once you leave the path, it is very difficult to return. It is rare that a private practice clinician can publish a sufficient amount and maintain the qualifications necessary for an academic position. However, it is relatively common for an academic to maintain solid clinical skills and enter into private practice. Not all academic physicians would succeed in private practice. However, overall, most academic physicians are qualified for both academics and private practice. Most private practice physicians are not qualified for academic positions.

3) Why would you limit yourself to only private practice? Twenty to 80 percent of jobs in any given field are academic, depending on the field, with the average hovering around 30 percent. You may have geographic considerations or family considerations down the road. But when you are first starting out, you should aim for as many job opportunities as possible. When I finished training in cardiac surgery, my wife was starting residency in radiology in St. Louis. Both are highly competitive fields. The only job for a cardiac surgeon in the region was at Saint Louis University. Thank goodness I was qualified! If I had gone down the private practice route, I am not sure how we would have figured it out. It is better to prepare yourself to be a candidate for as many jobs as possible when you are starting out.

4) God made man in his own image; humans, however, are less humble. We all say "It doesn't matter, you should choose the best career for you," and genuinely mean it. But we also feel a little better about ourselves when someone follows in our footsteps. Therefore if we have a "mini-me" vs. an anti-"mini-me," we choose the former. When you apply to residencies, all the people making decisions are, by definition, academic. Why would they choose to train someone who wanted to go into private practice? In some ways, it is a "failure" of that person to convince the trainee that the academic physician's career choice was "the best." Even if it is not a conscious choice, at best it is in the subconscious choice of every program director. At worst, if you are like me, I would only rank people who wanted to go into academics. Once again, put the shoe on the other foot. If you were a program director and choosing a candidate, would you want to choose someone holding the same vision of life that you do, or someone else?

5) The world is full of snobs. Many people, myself included, love to latch onto the reputation of top institutions. Even in private practice. While much of that "name recognition" is founded, much is unfounded. However, that "brand" often influences other patients and referring doctors. The better the reputation of your training institution, the better for you and your partners. My friend, a retina surgeon, practiced in the small Texas border town of Laredo. Because he had trained at Massachusetts Eye and Ear Infirmary, he was known as the "Harvard doctor." Promoted by all the local institutions as "the Harvard doctor," he had a wildly successful practice. To get to Harvard, he did everything I will discuss including building an extensive curriculum vitae that included many published articles. The last one he wrote was published the day he was accepted into fellowship. Afterward, he decided he would only do private practice; however he would have never had that opportunity if he had decided to go into private practice during medical school.

AN ALTERNATIVE PERSPECTIVE FROM
A DIVISION DIRECTOR OF GERIATRIC MEDICINE

Advice to Students

I advise young people going into medicine differently now than I did twenty or thirty years ago. Certainly the number one factor to consider now has to be lifestyle. You have to figure out what it is that can you do, at what requirements of time and work that will still allow you to have the lifestyle you want and a reasonable personal life.

Radiology and pathology are reasonably well-paying for example, and dermatology, now rising on lists of desirable specialties, can be lucrative. Then consider how hard you're prepared to work to get that position, and maintain it.

The second factor involves deciding whether you want to be an academic, or a clinician. If you want to be an academic, determine the best place that will accept you, will allow you to do research you enjoy and around which you can build a research program. If you want to be a really good clinician, then go to a place like the Cleveland Clinic that has a strong clinical program. I'd look for a relatively well known second tier program with good clinicians who will help you develop your clinical skills.

These early decisions concerning career are extraordinarily difficult for medical students who have not yet had much exposure to all the facets of medical life, and all the specialties. I encourage students to do one elective in areas they think they might be interested in, as it is very important to find out now if they're going to love it or hate it.

There are so many possibilities, now; the sky is the limit and you can do whatever you want, not just one thing. Find something you want to do and are reasonably good at it, maybe two, and then go and do them. If you're not enjoying what you do, change to something else—because why be unhappy?

Get Directions: Obtaining a Residency

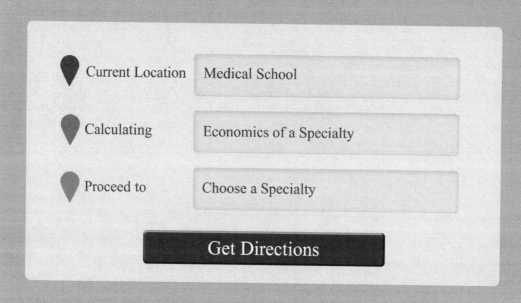

Current Location	Medical School
Calculating	Economics of a Specialty
Proceed to	Choose a Specialty

Get Directions

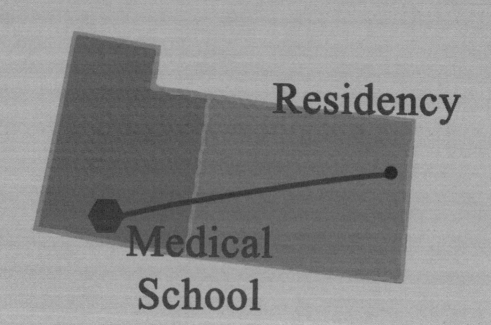

Choosing a Specialty

"Which field should I enter?"

This is a very difficult decision. It is a very personal one as well. My advice is to give the career an opportunity to choose you. Most students don't get a great deal of experience with specialties and subspecialties until rotations. Start early. Much like when you shadowed to evaluate your decision for entering medical school, get some hands on experience. Currently, I have a first year medical student shadowing me during his break. Good for him. If he likes cardiac surgery, great, if not, he can move on to another field. You can always change your mind. About 30 percent of physicians practice in a field other than the one that they started in. However, it is better to change your mind before you begin training. In general, while the differences between medicine and the surgical specialties are considerable, some surgical specialties, like orthopedics and ENT, contain a balance. The duration of the training should not be a factor. Whether your choice is internal medicine (three years) or cardiac surgery (six to ten years), after graduation the training all evens out. Really. If you want to be an interventional cardiologist, plan on three years of internal medicine plus three years of cardiology plus two years of interventional cardiology for a total of eight years of training. My wife did a one year internship plus four years in radiology plus one year in mammography plus one year as a clinical instructor, for a total of seven years. All that matters is that you do something you love.

I even believe that money evens out among specialists as well. According to the Bureau of Labor Statistics, among 45,000 general internists surveyed in 2012, the median income was $191,120 with an average wage of $92/hour. Median pay for a surgeon was $230,540 at $110/hour. At first, that seems like a big difference of $40,000 per year. However, after taxes that is reduced to about $30,000 per year, and much of that money may need to be spent on a babysitter. Generally, surgeons work more hours and take more frequent uncompensated call. Their training is usually longer and more intense, so much so that that they are unable to "moonlight" or work part time as many physicians in internal medicine or emergency medicine do for supplemental income both during and after training. Over the course of a career, there still may be some imbalance, but it in general incomes are more equal than they may appear on the surface.

Some specialties like cardiothoracic surgery seem to command extremely high incomes. For example, the American Medical Group Association reports a median income of $533,000 for cardiac and thoracic surgeons. However, because the training is longer and the hours more demanding during training and afterward, this specialty is typically limited to a one income family situation, wherein one spouse carries much of the non-family burden. In other fields that are less time intensive, it is much easier to coordinate a two income home. In addition, such intense specialties may offer little opportunity to earn additional income. For example, a new business model gaining traction in the medical field is the concept of the concierge practice, which offers better access to a limited number of patients by charging them $1,000 to $2,000 per year. A 500 patient practice, then, would yield $500,000 to $1,000,000 a year in income for the practice (excluding expenses.) In the end, I believe if anyone makes $1,000,000 per year, they usually work hard enough to *earn* at least $2,000,000. The trick is to understand that whatever area or specialty you choose, your career shouldn't be work at all.

By way of example, I'll share my own experience of how my wife and I came to choose as we did. I hope it helps.

I felt disconnected from my career path until I did third year rotations in medical school. After doing summer research in neurosurgery and realizing that I didn't enjoy it, I decided on a "lifestyle" residency. But a funny thing happened. While doing my third year rotations I realized I did not like what the physicians did in the "lifestyle" practices. I also realized that even if you only work 50 hours a week, 50 weeks a year, you'll have worked 2,500 hours. If your career is like most, in the 30 years after training you'll have put in close to 75,000 hours. That is a lot of time. I realized then that you'd better like what you do; otherwise, the rest of your life can't make up for it. I liked—I didn't love—the field of surgery. I didn't like the personalities of the surgeons I worked with, that was for sure. In retrospect, my initial dislike was the result of my immaturity and failure to understand the gravity of the field. But because I knew that I at least liked what they *did*, I decided to give it a try. I started General Surgery Training, had my first experience with cardiac surgery, and that was it; I fell in love with the field. After figuring out how to change my path and my direction, I was fortunate enough to make it work. I wish now that I had investigated cardiac surgery sooner. As it was, I ended up working much harder during training to catch up to my peers, most of whom had a substantially stronger foundation than I did.

My wife went into medical school to be a plastic surgeon. Because she had experience working in both the operating room and the emergency room, she already had significant exposure to orthopedic surgery and plastic surgery. While she was taking her science classes (she decided late and was on an alternate pathway), she volunteered to work with a plastic surgeon doing research. At that time, she decided that she wanted to treat breast cancer with both excision and reconstruction. She was on the right path. But at some point along the way, she decided that she didn't want to be a surgeon for multiple reasons, including that she also wanted to be the world's greatest mother. But she still wanted to treat breast cancer. Eventually she found radiology and went on to the field of mammography. All her hard work building a foundation and all her research and study paid off when she found and succeeded in the perfect field for her—even if mammography was a bit different from her original choice.

My wife and I are successful for many reasons. We work very hard. We are very good at what we do. But the number one reason for our success is that it never seems like we work a day in our lives. We love what we do. There are very few things I would choose to spend my time on other than work. Now that our children are growing up, we know the time we can spend with them is limited so we make it count. Whatever field you choose, make sure it is a passion rather than work. If you don't love it, leave it. It may take a while to find the right field; the path may prove difficult and even change. Start early and make frequent adjustments. Refuse to compromise on your career once you find it, and you and everyone around you will be much better off.

A word of caution. Not everyone is suited for every career. Right now, matching into cardiac surgery from medical school is highly competitive, and I would not have been a candidate when I graduated. My USMLE score alone would have not made the cut. If that is your case, i.e., your application is not competitive, there are other options. You may choose a different path to the same destination. For example, you can do general surgery and then cardiothoracic. You may decide to do internal medicine and eventually choose interventional cardiology instead of cardiac surgery, in which case there is a great deal of overlap. Your USMLE and experience may limit your choices. Do your best and most options will remain open. If you do your best and find some options close, work with a mentor to get closer to your goal.

AN ALTERNATIVE PERSPECTIVE FROM A MEDICAL STUDENT

On choosing a specialty

Students face considerable pressure to choose a residency field by our third year, when we've only had about half a year's exposure to all the specialties. Medical school is an environment that is prestigious in itself, that attracts leading specialists in their areas to teach a group of highly gifted and motivated people. This is very exciting and advantageous to students in a medical school setting, but may be somewhat limiting in terms of exposing us to all options.

Every specialist who comes in to lecture or teach is fiercely devoted to his field. Often they've done groundbreaking work in those fields so they naturally convey their enthusiasm and preference. But we don't often have general medicine people come in and talk about what they do—so students don't get much of a feeling for what being a urologist, an endocrinologist or a general practitioner would be like as a life. The result is that we feel a lot of pressure to go into a high-power specialty. Ideally, students would be exposed to more options and have more time to get to learn about them.

Then too, especially in the six year residency programs, it can be difficult to get off one path—especially in surgery—and segue to another, especially the lengthy integrated programs like cardiothoracic surgery. In some cases you'd have to reapply and redo some areas. If you do switch, then you're losing time since you're not academically productive. So there is a lot of pressure—which is why I think students need to make a concerted effort to shadow. Those who don't make the effort to shadow someone in a field they think they might be interested in are putting themselves at a disadvantage.

Very important in all this is making a serious effort early in medical school to really understand yourself, how you like to spend your time every day. Are you someone who is analytical, who likes to think deeply about things, figure things out and solve problems? Or do you prefer keeping busy, moving around and doing things with your hands? Or put other way, try to imagine how well you'd fit into this or that field as you move through your rotations—because by third year, you have to make a decision, so you need to have come to some conclusions. Above all, you want to do something that excites and engages you every single day.

Factors women face in choosing residencies

I know some women students who choose internal medicine over surgery even if they're interested in it, because they assume medicine will offer them a better shot at a more balanced life. Whether or not that's actually true, we don't know because we don't see many women role models in the surgical area. That's where I think mentoring could be very helpful, and it's something medical schools should address. For myself I am very aware of the tradeoffs a woman faces going into surgery, and have thought deeply about them.

The illusions vs. the realities of medical school

I think I was surprised at the sheer intensity of medical school, which I did not expect. Certainly we expected that the studying and the routine would be hard, but there is also an intense pressure to excel that blindsides many students. After all, your classmates are *all* super bright and competent. It's not like high school, where you've been way ahead of most of your peers.

To excel in a place like this is tougher than anything you've ever known, so it's easy to get down on yourself when you don't measure up to your own expectations. The stakes are high because they rest so heavily on the tangible results of your work here. Medicine attracts people who are used to achieving and then find themselves in situations where they might be rated "average" on a test or procedure. That's hard to take, but you have to come to terms with the pressure, remind yourself that you're here to help people—and then give yourself a break when you don't do so well once in a while. Accept that messing up occasionally is part of learning.

Most schools today do offer counseling and even courses in recognizing and managing stress. I think these are very valuable, and yet I think most students underutilize these resources for fear of an assumed stigma. They think they can do better, or tough it out. We talk about it in class sometimes, but seeking help is still considered something of a taboo.

AN ALTERNATIVE PERSPECTIVE FROM A CARDIOLOGY FELLOW

Choosing a specialty

I really don't know how people decide on a specialty; I do know it weighs heavily. For me, internal medicine secured my interest by the third year. By the end of a full year of internal medicine rotation—a standard rotation is two to six months—I'd had so much exposure to internal medicine that I felt very drawn to the field. I felt good about it, I was competent at it, and I liked the people I met in it. In hindsight, I think meeting key people in the field plays a huge role in deciding a specialty.

It's true that very few people are going into general practice anymore because they typically earn less given they have to carry the full burden of running an office with all the costs of staff, equipment and insurance. The evolution of the primary care physician over the last 30 years is such that the true professional who is in the office, always on call—is not there anymore. It's just an outdated concept of a physician.

I think most people are content to join group practices or otherwise work as employees of hospitals, or go the academic route. That way you don't have to go out and find patients; you only have to worry about doing what you're trained to do. The group or institution takes care of your credentialing and your insurance; there are more of you to take call and your hours are more regular.

That said, I'm seeing a real transition in the kinds of career choices younger residents are making now. My parents' generation was all about working really hard, getting good jobs and saving a lot of money. Then you saw a generation that seemed all about making as much money as they could, doing whatever procedure would generate the highest fees. I think both those models are fading out. Now I'm seeing people make choices centered in balancing their interests and their personal lives. For example, emergency medicine is a very hot specialty now, and both radiology and dermatology are popular and competitive.

Yes, you have student debt to pay off, but you know that going in. With some management, it's not crippling. I'm not worried about it too much, because I think that if you get through school and into your field and you like the work, you're going to be able to pay your debt off.

Choosing a specialty

In medical school I found that I liked the physiology of cardiology. I knew I was going to do internal medicine, and for some reason cardiology was always in the back of my mind. Then when I started rotating through it I found I enjoyed the practice; I felt it was exciting and important to people's lives. Certainly cardiac disease represents probably the largest disease burden in the US and the world today.

Cardiology entails pretty standard diseases, and the field has the benefit of having a vast patient population to study. No field has had more clinical trials, which means we have tremendous knowledge now of how to treat patients and improve their lives and long term outcomes. Now, if we provide a therapy, we can be really confident that it works. Because we can study it so well, we understand this disease better than we understand many others; and because of all the medications we now have, heart attacks are going down.

Choosing a residency

Most medical schools are keen to place their graduates appropriately, and our program was helpful, very student oriented. It was very common for me to talk to my chairman of medicine, who would sit down with me, look at records and scores, and help me determine the best possibilities. Yes, these are good opportunities but don't waste your time looking at those, and so on. In internal medicine, most states have multiple programs, so we could pick and choose as we liked. If we applied to a top tier medicine program we had a good chance of getting in; but in something like cardiothoracic surgery we could only apply to a few highly competitive programs and hope.

Advice to young people going into medicine

As for advice to young people entering medicine, I'd say pick a field you really like. Don't pick a field just for the lifestyle or the compensation. Choose something you like because if in twenty years you're not getting paid what you once were—and you're doing something you hate—you can't retrain in something else at that point. The most important thing early on is to be open, and find what you're passionate about. I've heard so many stories from people who say, "I came to medical school to be a neurosurgeon and now I'm an ortho guy."

It's important to look at many areas, try a few of them, and talk to people all along the way; because you won't be able to be a good doctor unless you have lots of experiences that help you grow as a person.

Get Directions: Obtaining a Residency

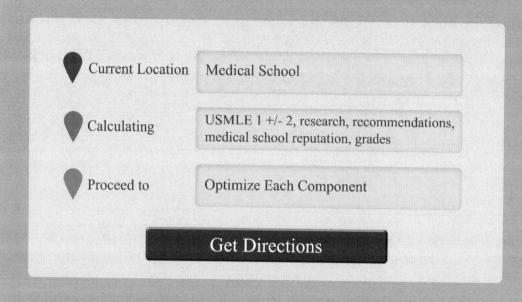

Current Location	Medical School
Calculating	USMLE 1 +/- 2, research, recommendations, medical school reputation, grades
Proceed to	Optimize Each Component

Get Directions

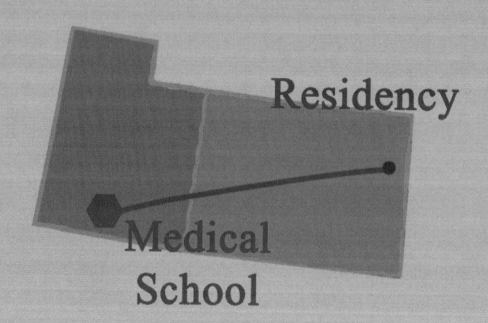

Residency

Medical School

Qualifications for Residency

Each of these components will influence your application for residency, regardless of the field you choose. Some fields will be more competitive than others. The components outlined below will determine your candidacy for each field.

Standardized Tests

You cannot escape! These tests are the only means by which to really compare individuals from different institutions. The United States Medical Licensing Examination (USMLE) is a multi-part professional exam sponsored by the National Board of Medical Examiners and the Federation of State Medical Boards. The test is comprised of four components: USMLE Step 1, USMLE Step 2 CK, USMLE Step 2 CS and USMLE Step 3. Each yields a different score taken at different points in your career. All MDs must pass all steps before they are able to practice in the USA. All DOs either must pass all USMLE steps, or pass the multi-part Comprehensive Osteopathic Medical Licensing Examination (COMLEX). Students who have graduated from medical schools outside the US and Canada must pass all three steps of the USMLE to be licensed to practice in the US. However, if you are going to apply for an MD-based residency, expect to take the USMLE.

USMLE step 1 is taken after the first two years, and covers the first two years of curricula. It is an eight-hour computer-based exam consisting of 322 multiple choice questions (MCQs) divided into seven blocks, each consisting of 46 questions covering pathology, pharmacology, physiology, microbiology, biochemistry, anatomy, behavioral science, nutrition, genetics and aging. No matter how hard or easy a school is, the USMLE offers an opportunity for level comparison of students from different schools. Once again, it is really up to you to get the best score that you can get. The USMLE Step 1 was the second hardest test I ever took after cardiac surgery written boards. Overall pass rates for first time USMLE Step 1 test takers are: 96% for US MD medical school graduates, 92% for US DO osteopathic medical school graduates, and

76% for international medical school graduates. If you fail, you can take it again, but *don't* fail. You will have to answer and explain why forever; you can't keep it a secret. Once you pass, you are done. The passing score you receive is final so it is in your best interest to excel on the first try. Most programs require that you pass prior your clinical rotations.

Average Step 1 scores for various residencies are available in "Charting Outcomes in the Match" via the National Resident Matching Program each year. This information will help you evaluate your candidacy for a specific field in real time.

Some students are naturally better at taking these tests than other students. Too bad! It is up to you to figure out how to do your best. I do have a few hints, however, and many of them overlap with the other standardized tests.

1) Study like you mean it! Block out time to prepare for these tests. No TV, no music, etc. Test administrators allow no distractions during the test, so avoid them when you study. Create an environment similar to the test every time you study, so it won't freak you out when you take it. You will be used to it.

2) You can never start too early. Don't make the mistake of cramming. It is too important and should be something you work on over your entire medical school career. I recommend studying from the review books as a supplement as you are learning the material. For example, while you are studying for anatomy, use a USMLE review book as a supplement. Make notes in your review book. Organize and save materials that are useful from your coursework for easy access later on. That way, you will become familiar with the format of the subject as it's presented on the test. Consider it a useful aid by which you can do additional questions and problems in real time as they relate to your classes. But recognize most schools grade on "Honors," "Pass" and "Fail." If you are likely to achieve "Pass" rather than "Honors," the school-specific materials are less important than your preparation for the boards.

3) Re-review the materials and take practice tests on weekends and breaks. Obviously, you will be very busy, and intense study is hard to work into your day. However, the materials are light. Bring a book on the train. Review flashcards while you're standing in line, waiting for a class to start, or doing laundry. Make study a part of your day. The more you review the materials and the more times you work through the problems, the better prepared you will

be. I have taken over 15 of these national tests (from ACT to Cardiothoracic Board re-certification). Initially, I wasn't a big fan of practice questions. But the more difficult the tests became, the more I began to appreciate the value of those questions. Because the number of concepts considered testable is finite, many of the questions feature topics that show up on every exam. I would recommend doing as many questions as many times as possible. It is important to understand why the correct answer is correct, and equally important to understand why the incorrect answers are not. However, it is easier to figure out what to study if you already know the question or topic of focus (another example of "start from the end"). If you review the same material from the same study aids over and over, it gives you the best chance of doing well. Consistent repetition is the only way to master the complex material that you will be expected to learn and retain.

4) Although many students do not consider the option, I recommend taking a formal test prep class. If you decide to do so, make sure that you have ample time before the test date. The test prep classes, such as those offered by Kaplan, have clearly demonstrated a difference in the test scores of students who take them. There are several and I do not endorse any particular one. Unlike the MCAT, it is difficult to take these classes until after you have seen the material. The best time to take the class is right before boards. The amount of material is overwhelming and the amount of memorization unlike any other I've experienced.

5) You will not be able to retake the test just to improve your score; you can only retake it if you fail it. Be ready the first time.

USMLE Step 2

Step 2 is designed to assess whether medical school students or graduates can apply medical knowledge, skills and understanding of clinical science essential for provision of patient care under supervision. US medical students typically take Step 2 during the fourth year of medical school. It is not required for residency application, but a passing score is required to begin residency. Some students who do not perform to expectations on Step 1 try to perform better on Step 2 to compensate. Overall, this is a bad strategy. Not everyone is going to have a Step 2 when they apply to residency, so the comparison is not very useful. If you are well below the bar on Step 1, nothing will make up for it. If you are on the fence, research and recommendations will be more powerful. Spend your time on those. Not everyone agrees, but as I have said, this advice is mine, take it or leave it.

Step 2 is further divided into two separate exams. USMLE Step 2 CK is designed to assess clinical knowledge through a traditional, multiple choice examination. It is a nine-hour exam consisting of eight one hour long blocks, each comprised of approximately 44 questions. The subjects covered in this exam are clinical sciences like medicine, surgery, pediatrics, psychiatry and obstetrics & gynecology. USMLE Step 2 CS is designed to assess clinical skills through simulated patient interactions in which each examinee engages with 12 standardized patients (SP) portrayed by actors. The examinee has 15 minutes to complete a full history taking and a clinical examination for each patient, and then 10 more minutes to write a patient note describing the findings, initial differential diagnosis list and a list of initial tests. Administration of the Step 2-CS began in 2004. The examination is only offered in five cities across the country: Atlanta, Chicago, Houston, Los Angeles, and Philadelphia.

After the match, all that matters is that you have passed all the USMLE steps. Your step scores will never again have any significance. However, how well you do on these tests often reflects the strength of your foundation as you enter the field of your choice.

USMLE Step 3 is the final exam in the USMLE series. Successful completion is required for permanent state licensure. The test is designed to assess whether a medical school graduate can apply medical knowledge and understanding of biomedical and clinical science essential for the unsupervised practice of medicine. Typically, this exam is taken at the end of the first year of residency. Foreign medical graduates can take Step 3 before starting residency in about ten US states. Step 3 is a 16-hour examination divided over two days; each day of testing must be completed within eight hours. The first day consists of seven blocks with 336 multiple-choice items; the second day consists of four blocks with 144 multiple choice items, as well as 12 Clinical Case Simulations.

Again, from my perspective, *no one will ever ask your Step 3 score*. A pass is as valuable as the highest score in the country, so spend your time on the other components and on mastering your specialty.

Research

The basic tenets of research are the same as in the prior section, but the level of importance increases substantially at this stage. Everyone who wants a career in medicine should do research. Success in research is measured by two metrics only: the quantity and quality of publications achieved and amount of dollars in research grants accrued. As mentioned previously, the steps toward publication are generally as follows: hypothesis, study design, protocol submission to Institutional Review Board (IRB), request for change from IRB X1-3, IRB resubmission, IRB approval, data acquisition, data analysis, manuscript preparation, sending to co-authors, revision after coauthor review, submission to journal, rejection/request for revision, revision of manuscript, re-submission, eventual acceptance. The process is formidable and even intimidating, but once you go through it a few times, your value as a contributor and a potential asset to a researcher increases markedly. Unless you have demonstrated that you have participated in the entire process, your value to a researcher will be limited.

A great goal for this step is to have one to three papers published by application to residency. Any authorship, any journal, any subject is useful, but at this stage, it would be best to have one or two in the field to which you are applying. Publishing two articles related to your field will impress far more favorably than the excuse I hear from 95 percent or more of applicants: "Well, it was really interesting research, but it didn't work out as we planned." On paper, not having any publications is indistinguishable from not engaging in research at all.

You can do other small, easy projects at the same time. Unpublished work has value, even if infinitely less than a single publication. Generally, you will end up working on three or four papers in order to get one published. I have published over 70 papers in peer-reviewed journals, which means that I've worked on about 300. As you get more experienced, your ratio should improve. For example, by now almost everything I write will get published, in part because I no longer work on projects that are unlikely to get published. I am much more efficient with my time. However, once you successfully publish, the paper is yours for life and will always be a line on your CV. Add five lines a year and in ten years you will have 50 publications. In 20 years you will have 100. If you don't start now, you will likely still have none.

The second component is funding. This is also a lifelong process that you need to start now. Multitudes of scholarships, grants and other means of financial aid are available to medical students from sources ranging from local medical schools to national specialty societies. Get some! Securing aid will not only start your experience with the application process but also demonstrate your ability to succeed. I have fallen off the track in this aspect. Though successful in obtaining funding in medical school and residency, I've only achieved funding from industry as an attending, in part because of my environment. Ideally, I would have already received National Institute of Health (or equivalent) funding. I am actively working to correct this. Securing funding doesn't happen overnight, but it does begin early. At your level, I would be willing to work for free until you get some experience. Choose to work for someone who has already received NIH funding, and demonstrated that he provides opportunities for students to work on grants. Once you gain experience and prove that you are capable of obtaining national funding, you'll be valuable to an institution and more competitive for academic jobs.

Recommendations and Personal Connections

At this point, recommendations are very important. They are even more important for fellowship training after residency, when the USMLE scores are virtually irrelevant, and outstanding recommendations expected. Who you know becomes increasingly important in fields that suddenly become very small. I will share a scenario that I have created for medical students and give you my belief.

I am a program director for an integrated cardiac surgery residency. I have two candidates that I am considering. Mike has a letter from the dean of Johns Hopkins, a radiologist by training, who declares that Mike is the single greatest potential surgeon he has ever seen. Mike is the embodiment of Halsted, DeBakey, Cooley and Sabiston (all iconic surgeons) combined. It would be a grave mistake if I don't take him.

Jean has a letter from a friend I trained with. My friend says that Jean is a solid resident who will do a good job. He says that she is a hard worker. She won't be the best resident I ever trained, but she won't let me down. He would take her if he had a training program and will take it as a personal favor if I took her in mine.

Which applicant would you accept: Mike or Jean?

For me, the choice is simple. I would take Jean. The dean is not a surgeon. How can he predict what makes a surgeon? More importantly, I don't know him. If he is wrong and Mike is a dud, I have no means of repercussion. If Jean is a dud, my friend is not my friend and I will remind him of it every time I see him at every surgery meeting. Every opportunity I get, I will let others in our field know not to trust him. If he endorses a candidate, his reputation is at stake. Moreover, if I have any questions, I can call him on the phone and believe him.

Now, it is difficult to figure out exactly who knows who, but the general patterns are simple. Residency program directors all have annual meetings. They all know one another. Most people know chairmen. Every specialty has one or two major societies. Each one of these societies has a journal and a leadership board. Those serving on the editorial board of the journal or as elected officials in one of these societies, are well known to almost everyone. A good letter from one or more of those individuals can lend considerable meaning to an application. In addition, applicants should check where their attending physicians completed training. A letter from an alumnus will carry some weight with the admissions committee at the institution they attended.

Getting to know these individuals is easy. Approach them in your first year. Ask their advice. Make sure you rotate with them and do an outstanding job. It is better if you establish a relationship with the early. I would do research with them in my first year of medical school and beyond. The medical students with whom I have published and witnessed clinically receive incredible letters and support from me. Those that do a mediocre job on a short rotation can expect the appropriate level of support.

Away rotations

I highly encourage them. My suggestion is that you choose an institution that you think you may want to attend with well-known faculty. At the very least, you can obtain another strong letter from a known individual. At best, if they are like me, they will only strongly consider you if they have had the opportunity to observe you clinically. I personally thought this aspect critical when I was ranking people.

Medical School's Reputation

This is fixed. Nothing you can do about it at this point. Recognize that while this is not as important as all the above factors, it does matter, especially if it is a top institution. Fortunately, reputation is not critical. Even a great institution like Harvard doesn't make up for a mediocre USMLE or lack of publications. If I had a candidate who went to the worst medical school in the country, but who had a 99 percentile on Step 1, rotated on my service and done a great job, *and* 15 publications—I would rank him first.

Grades. I believe grades are overrated. Grades are impressive if you are AOA (alpha omega alpha, top 20 percent), but not as impressive as a 95 percentile Step 1. If you are applying for surgery, getting only a high pass but not an honors ranking is a bit concerning, but not if someone I know writes you a great letter and vouches for you. Don't underperform and barely pass, but don't sweat it if you can't hit "honors."

AN ALTERNATIVE PERSPECTIVE FROM A MEDICAL STUDENT

The importance of mentors

Mentors, I think, are as a concept probably underutilized by students. Having a mentor is absolutely essential to a med student, and I found having one I can go to has been pivotal in helping me decide what I want to go into. However, so far I've found little in the medical school experience that encourages students to seek out a mentor. You may feel okay about approaching a doctor or professor about the specialty or some aspect of research, but not about other areas that we all think about like balancing the personal and professional aspects of a career.

I am aware that some medical schools do make a concerted effort to organize and support mentoring programs, actually matching professors and attending doctors with students. The idea is to establish ongoing relationships over the entire school experience and in some cases beyond into residency programs. But ultimately it all hinges on the individual relationship between the mentor and the student. Students need to follow up on that because ideally such a relationship will last years.

AN ALTERNATIVE PERSPECTIVE FROM A CARDIOLOGY FELLOW

The importance of a mentor

A mentor is definitely a major element in your medical education, and in some cases, I think a mentor can be the defining element. A mentor who can guide you can make all the difference between burning out and quitting early.

I've had several good mentors who've made a huge difference in my life. One mentor was special for being a kind of career guide with whom I could discuss programs and the types of things I might want to look at when I was applying. He was assigned to me by the school, which ran an excellent "docent" program. Assigned in our third year when we started doing continuity clinic, or outpatient clinic, our docents stayed with us through the remaining four years. In our fourth year we started going onto the inpatient service, so that one month out of that year we'd be working with that attending.

Because my docent got to watch my development as I learned, he came to know me pretty well. I don't think traditional medical school programs tend to offer something like this, or they do, but assign mentors randomly, which may or may not work very well. Ideally, mentors should be sought out. My mentor was crucial to my development. I think I would have been someone who didn't do well if I'd not had him in my life at that time.

Get Directions: Obtaining a Residency

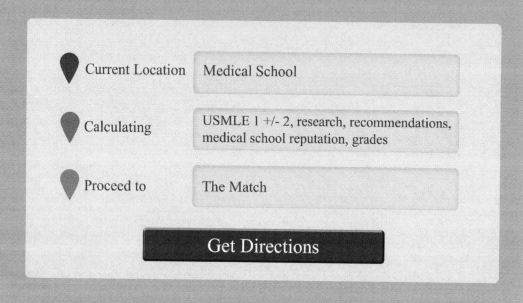

Current Location — Medical School

Calculating — USMLE 1 +/- 2, research, recommendations, medical school reputation, grades

Proceed to — The Match

Get Directions

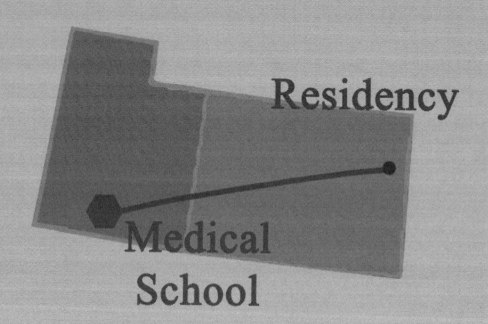

Residency

Medical School

Tips for "The Match"

Given the abundance of readily available information about "the match," which deserves a separate book, I will address its intricacies only briefly here.

Most ACGME residency positions go through a matching a system that is based on a central standardized application process for more than 20 specialties. Each individual applicant chooses a number of programs in a specific field and applies. The program decides whether or not to interview the candidate. Generally they interview 10 to15 candidates for every position. The candidate travels to interviews at his/her own expense and ranks the programs he/she would like to attend from favorite to least favorite. The programs do the same in ranking their candidates. A computer program then "matches" the choices of the candidates with those of the respective programs, and on "Match Day" applicants around the country receive notice of the results. It is a very stressful, but fair system. Here are a few tips for applicants that may prove helpful.

1) Rank the programs with the best reputations highest unless you do not think you will fit in. The best way to figure out the reputations is by looking at the journals and seeing who is on the leadership of the specialty society and the journal's editorial board. You will notice a very disproportionate amount of power concentrated over relatively few institutions. I trained at Washington University in Saint Louis and the Cleveland Clinic. I am now at Saint Louis University. In cardiac surgery, I could not have done better. There are many similar institutions, but not *that* many. Every field is unique and different, so be sure to check out each one.

2) If you are planning additional training, choose a program with a track record for placement into that specialty.

3) Rank programs that place people into good jobs, particularly academic ones.

4) Have your mentor call one or two programs on your behalf.

5) Apply to about a third of the programs you know to be "a stretch" with your grades, a third for which you know you'd be a good candidate, and a third you know to be a "sure thing" acceptance. Be advised, however, that nothing is "sure" during the match.

6) Avoid preliminary positions. They almost never lead anywhere.

7) A categorical position at the worst program in the country is better than a preliminary at the best. You can always consider transfer later, but you will be more marketable if you have categorical spot.

8) Not matching is a stigma that is very difficult to overcome.

9) If you are a marginal candidate for your field, apply in another one for which you are a good candidate as well. It is expensive, but it would be easier to prove yourself in the other field. For example, if you are poor candidate for surgery but want to do cardiac surgery, I would apply for internal medicine as well. If you don't match in surgery but do match in internal medicine, complete it. You can prove yourself during training and then go into surgery. It is only an extra three years. You may change your mind and instead apply for training in cardiology. If at the end of three years that does not work out, you still have training that makes you employable. On the other hand, not matching and doing two or three preliminary years, although occasionally successful, usually just wastes time. And does not help you advance your career.

Get Directions: Obtaining a Residency

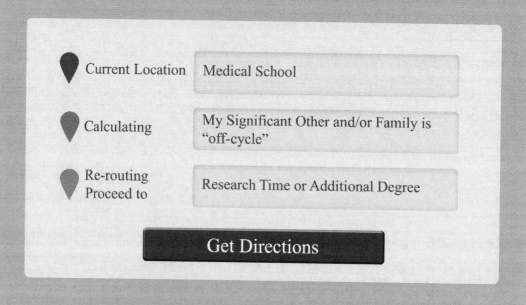

Current Location — Medical School

Calculating — My Significant Other and/or Family is "off-cycle"

Re-routing Proceed to — Research Time or Additional Degree

Get Directions

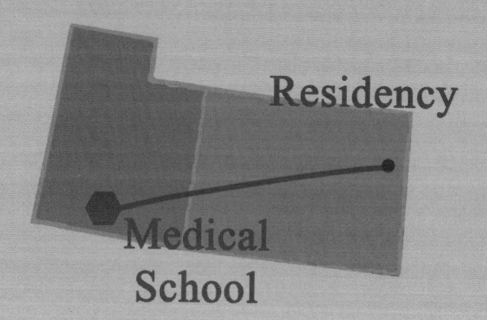

Residency

Medical School

Managing "Off-cycle" Careers

The incidence of conflicting job and training opportunities between spouses or partners both working toward medical careers is not uncommon. In our case, I was in training while my wife was in medical school. I had matched in a two-year cardiothoracic training program, but she was going to graduate in the beginning of my second year. This would leave us "off-cycle." Because I would be finishing while she was going to be a second year resident, coordinating a job in a single location was going to be difficult.

The question then became: what would she do with that period of time? Rather than taking on the stigma of "a year off" after graduation, my wife decided to delay her graduation a year. She did research for that year in St. Louis where I was in training, and in her fourth year did most of her rotations "away" in St. Louis. By the time she applied for residency, she was a *more* competitive candidate because of her research experience. Ultimately we were able to get a job and residency together at the same time.

Other options include additional degrees, like an MBA, MPH or JD. Pursuing any one of these degrees gives you a window of one to three years that will not only get you "on cycle," but also make you a more valuable candidate. However, if you try to pursue this pathway after you graduate, you will raise questions that require explanation. Often residency program directors don't take the time to ask and just select a candidate who is finishing medical school.

AN ALTERNATIVE PERSPECTIVE FROM A FEMALE ASSISTANT PROFESSOR

Managing two residencies in two different places

Coordinating two residencies and/or fellowships requires planning and a certain amount of serendipity if they're in the same city; but pulling this off when the two partners are training in different locations, especially if children are involved, takes logistical skills and sheer willpower.

Given our different specialties, my husband and I went through two years pretty much apart while he trained in Chicago and I trained in St. Louis. We made a lot of six hour drives back and forth between the two cities with two young children in the back seat just so we could have some family time together. It was difficult, but with some planning, doable and so worth it. In the end, we were lucky that we both found jobs we love in the same city once we finished training.

Get Directions: Obtaining a Residency

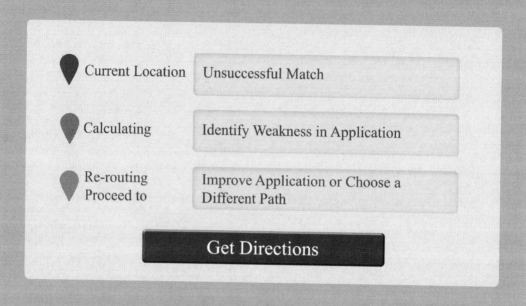

Current Location	Unsuccessful Match
Calculating	Identify Weakness in Application
Re-routing Proceed to	Improve Application or Choose a Different Path

Get Directions

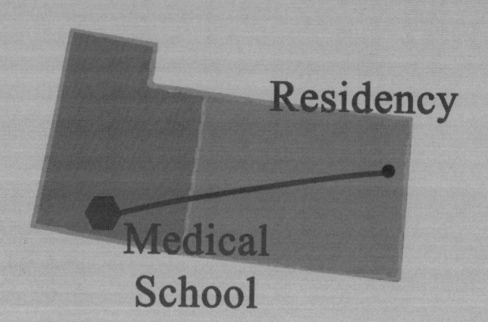

Residency

Medical School

Unsuccessful Match

If you are unlucky, or unrealistic, you may not receive a residency position. Whether a graduate of a US or international medical school, you will find that taking the advice I have outlined will serve you well in getting you back on a path to success. To reiterate, let's review as follows.

1) Avoid preliminary positions. They almost never lead anywhere. If you are in one, try to get *any* categorical position in any field.

2) A categorical position at the worst program in the country is better than a preliminary position at the best. You can always consider a transfer of programs or specialty later.

3) Leaving the clinical realm and going into research at this point is usually a one-way road away from clinical medicine. The more time off from clinical, the more concerns program directors have. The transition back can be rough and dangerous.

4) If you are a marginal candidate for your chosen field, apply to another field in which you are a good candidate as well. It is expensive, but it would be easier to prove yourself in the other field. For example, as I previously mentioned for marginal candidates entering the match, if you are poor candidate for surgery but want to do cardiac surgery, apply for internal medicine as well. If you don't match in surgery but do match in internal medicine, complete it. You can prove yourself during training and then go into cardiology. If, at the end of three years, those options don't work out, you still have training that makes you employable. On the other hand, not

matching and doing two or three preliminary years, although occasionally successful, usually just wastes time. For example, if you do three years of preliminary PGY1, best case scenario, it will count as one year. Likely, you will need to repeat it as a categorical resident anyway.

5) Plan on a much longer training program than your peers. There is no way to "shave" time. If you are in a preliminary spot and are lucky enough to get a categorical spot, embrace the opportunity to repeat a year. You should be better than the other interns and can use some of the "extra" time for research.

6) Training outside of the US doesn't count. Don't try to make it count.

Get Directions: Succeeding in Residency

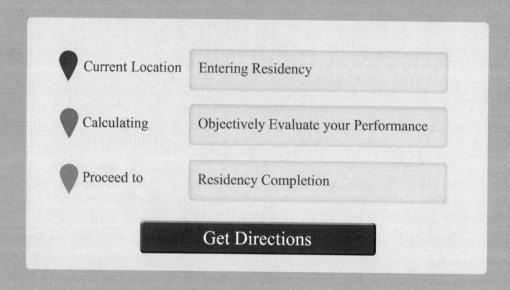

Current Location	Entering Residency
Calculating	Objectively Evaluate your Performance
Proceed to	Residency Completion

Get Directions

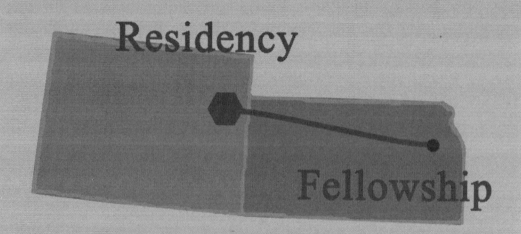

Residency

Fellowship

Succeeding in Residency

Residency may take from three years to a decade. Not everyone finishes, and not everyone leaves on a positive note. Each residency and each resident is unique, but some general rules apply.

1) Enjoy the privilege. As a resident you are busier than you can imagine. You become fatigued. It is easy to let cynicism creep in. Don't. When I was a resident, I was complaining to my cousin one holiday. "You know, about 60 percent of my job is like playing video games. It is great. I get to help people and it is fun. But I fill out so much paperwork, the attendings expect so much, I need to work so hard, etc. etc." After about 20 minutes of complaining, my cousin smiled, looked me straight in the eye and said, "Rick, I am an accountant for a top five firm. What percent of my day do you think I spend helping people? What percent of my day is like playing video games, do you think?" Point taken. I never complained again. However, I should have spent a little more time appreciating what a great gift my patients gave me. I learned while I helped them. What a privilege. Helping them allowed me to help so many other people, including family and friends down the road. Enjoy that privilege during training.

2) Earn and maintain the confidence of your colleagues and supervising physicians. Like anything else, it is easier to build and maintain this up front than it is to blow it and try to re-establish. Start by doing due diligence to those before you and establish their expectations for you up front. For example, if you are going into a residency program, contact former and current residents to learn about expectations among the various attending physicians, nurses and residents. When I was a cardiac fellow we had a

book of physician preferences that helped. Look up the curriculum vitae of your teachers and read their articles. You should know what topics they have published on.

3) Recognize that about half of the work you do should be outside of the hospital. At this point, you should be an adult learner. You are working with physicians who trained prior to the 80 hour work week. Moreover, you need to take responsibility for self-directed learning. It is not only an ACGME requirement; it is a practice that you will need to continue after your training. Medicine is a rapidly evolving field. Much of what you learn in training will be outdated as you practice. Learning how to keep learning is perhaps the most critical skill you will need to acquire. Don't ask a basic question. Ask an adult question. By that I mean, if you can answer the question, look it up yourself; then ask one you can't look up. Recognize that the other residents and attending physicians are teaching assistants, not textbooks. You will benefit from this approach. If they give you basic answers, you won't remember them anyway. If you look them up yourself, you are more likely to remember them long-term. Quite honestly, sometimes your attending will not always be right either.

4) Be a good partner to your co-residents. They will be in your field a long time. Any poor treatment during training will be remembered for your entire career. Remember, they may be in a position to help you later on. Strive to establish a reputation that will make them inclined to help.

5) Recognize that your evaluations and reputation will not only depend on the opinion of your program director or "the chief", but all those with whom you work. Nurses, physician extenders, other residents, in short, all those around you will be discussing your performance both formally and informally. If you always try your best and maintain your professionalism at all times, it will pay off in the long run.

6) Be a good citizen. Be the first to arrive and the last to leave. Don't make others wait for you. If there is any opportunity to volunteer for a task, do so. Don't whine or complain. None of that will benefit you in the long run. Again, put the "shoe on the other foot." What behaviors would you like from the ideal resident? Be that person, as best you can.

7) Residency is hard. You will have to make many choices. There is no room for behaviors or drama that will impair your performance. Save your partying for vacations. Consider using part of your vacation for research and study.

8) You will be under constant evaluation. Your weakest moment is the one that will define you. Always be at your best.

An Alternative Perspective from an Experienced Nurse Manager

What doctors-in-training can learn from nurses

The dominant illusion incoming residents have is that they're going to call all the shots and they're going to do every procedure they expect to do. I'll see them with a piece of equipment and say, "Where're you going with that?" They are not above reprimand. They need to ask questions and they need to wait their turn because they don't know everything.

The first thing a resident should do on coming into the department is to find out who the nursing leader is. In my experience, that leader will want to share information residents need to know, such as what standards they're expected to meet, what protocols they're expected to know and follow, and so on. Then they should find out who the nursing educators are and make plans to spend a couple of hours with them so they can learn their skills and abilities, and the specifics of their role in what is really a holistic system of care.

The practitioner in my department meets with her team at the start of each month's rotation to give students and residents a handbook of department guidelines our chief wants them to follow, how he wants things done with what drips, lines and medications and so on. I urge them to embrace these, because following them can prevent them from having to make a late night call to the chief when something goes awry and having to admit "Oh-oh, here's where I am and I'm not sure how I got here."

From the beginning residents should work hard to create relationships with the nurses, because they're the ones they'll rely on to prevent them from creating a crisis. I'd like to see residents shadow a nursing preceptor or charge nurse at least four hours a day when they first start on the floor. Doing so would help them a lot to learn skills and procedures, build rapport and create relationships. Typically when they come in new, you'll start to explain something and they respond with "I already know that," cutting off the very information supply line they need.

However, even if they've heard it before, they will gain something new in hearing it again from a highly experienced voice. Residents need to be able to *listen*—and then, make a decision.

When nurses know residents are tuning them out, they do the same. They will protect their patient, but they will let you hang yourself when the attending calls. They'll be able to answer for what they know, but they won't be able to help you with what *you* should know. I can assure you that you do *not* want to be the resident on the phone when the attending calls and says "I need to talk to the nurse."

On qualities residents need to become great doctors

Two of the most important qualities a young doctor can develop are humility, and the ability to sit and listen. One of the most remarkable residents we had in our program here would sit at the bedside and listen to silly banter sometimes, to create a deep personal relationship with the patient. It was never inappropriate; he was just there, present, interested. He spent the hours he had in the unit and on the floor where he was going to be assigned, *learning*, and that included visiting his patients and listening to them. Every day he learned something new.

What I really noticed was that he sat down *with* his patients, at eye level. He'd get down on one knee to talk to a patient's husband, who was seated. The implied message was: "I may have bad information to tell you but this is why I'm here—to sit with you, explain to you, share your journey and your decision."

This skill set—the ability to bond with your patients—is crucial to being a successful doctor, whether in private or academic practice. It's not uncommon for patients to turn doctors off. They'll say "I don't want that guy in here again." So then you've lost it all, your conversation, your ability to get the clinical information you need from that patient to exercise your critical and clinical thinking. Listening is crucial because if the patient doesn't tell you things, you don't know what's wrong.

Understanding what nurses do

Nurses' duties are increasing in their variety and importance, in that we're getting away from some of the bedside things we used to do, and hiring other people to do them. For example, there was a time when the patient left the floor for physical therapy, and then came back to the floor where the nurse would do the follow-up exercises at the bedside. Now physical therapists come to the floor to work with patients at the bedside—which frees up nurses for other functions.

Nurses also perform many more administrative tasks than before, due to the increase in federal guidelines. We have to do a lot more documentation to protect the patient and to show we're adhering to patient safety guidelines. For example the doctor may write the order for restraints, but the nurse is responsible for making sure that order is followed exactly, so that patient doesn't get injured, and for documenting both the order and compliance.

The pace of performance nurses face—making sure we're taking care of multiple issues like sterility, reducing infections, reducing the number of days a patient has a central line, etc.—is also daunting. Often we're asked to do things right in the moment, and sometimes that's not possible. But the government or any outside body can come in and look to see what we've done or haven't. If they see a conflict, they'll question it.

Documentation has improved now that we've gone from paper to online notation. Our hospital has installed rolling computers, so as physicians are rounding the residents are at the computer, pulling up information. For the nurse, sharing computers with doctors can be problem. If she's really busy, it might be four o'clock in the afternoon before she can chart for the whole day; but in a court of law it looks like she did her 8 a.m. assessment at 4 p.m. Nurses get very annoyed when doctors come in and take over computers, and then I have to go break up a fight.

Our greatest problem with incoming residents is that they don't see nursing's function as collaborative. In the beginning, they seem to think that nurses are not critical thinkers; that they are there to take orders and do tasks like getting patients up and to the bathroom. But nurses who work in ICU and on the floor have to have extraordinary critical thinking skills or they couldn't do their work, which entails assessing what's going on with their patients at all times.

The way doctors and nurses interact is changing because the way we deliver care is changing. Many hospitals now emphasize the "patient experience." Patients now get questionnaires that ask things like "Did the doctors speak directly to you? Did he explain the procedure?" Part of that kind of care begins in the relationship between the nurse and the doctor, in front of the patient. The doctor should speak to both rather than one and then the other. If there is a question in handling a patient's care then doctors, residents and nurses respond as a group. The emphasis is on collaboration of care at all levels.

AN ALTERNATIVE PERSPECTIVE FROM A FEMALE ASSISTANT PROFESSOR

Residency: expectations vs. reality

Medical school proved all I expected it to be in terms of difficulty and pressure. Residency, however, was much harder than I imagined, and I don't think most residents are prepared for the intensity. It's not that the material is too hard or the learning too demanding. It's coming in to work *every single day* and facing long hours on duty without a break that wear you down.

In my case, there would be weeks and weeks that I wouldn't get a day off. You can do that for a month, two months or three, but six years of such a schedule is very stressful and draining. Many residencies have since changed their on-call policies, but it was extremely difficult at the time, and quite often a shock to residents. So you do need to build in some coping strategies and be very vigilant about guarding your time.

The intensity of residency can also be isolating, so be prepared to accept that some social isolation is going to happen once you start training. One thing I noticed early on was that my girlfriends, other than those I'd known in medical school, began to drop me because I wasn't available. Ever.

In fact, not only do your friends drop you—your family drops you! I had to miss a number of family occasions that were important to me, like my cousin's wedding, which fell on the first day of internship and there was just *no way* I could go there for it. Holidays were challenging because my husband and I could never get enough time off to travel and be with family. Very often it was just the four of us here for Christmas because we couldn't get time off. I was used to sharing holidays with family, and wanted my girls to have that experience too.

Expect that friends and family will ask you to come to this or that and you will have to say no, and then accept that when you say no four, five, and six times they will stop asking. Your relationships with family and friends can and do erode. In training, there is not a lot you can do about this except to be prepared that you'll be making compromises in your family's life along the way, and to prepare them all as well.

Having Children

My situation was a little different from most of my peers, in that I had my first child in my first year of medical school, and my second in my last year of medical school. Of course this is highly unusual; most women wait until residency to have their children, but then there is no perfect time in a medical career to have a baby. For male medical students, having a baby with their wives is certainly harder than not having one, but their lives are less disrupted than women's are.

Having our children early actually worked out well for us because while medical school keeps you very busy with studies, it allows you a little more flexibility in time. Residency, which requires you to be at work every single day, offers no flexibility whatsoever. Our children

126

were here by residency, so we did not have to deal with the stresses of pregnancy and maternity leave in that period. That said, we did encounter plenty of challenges.

AN ALTERNATIVE PERSPECTIVE FROM A CARDIOLOGY FELLOW

Making the Most of Training

When I arrived for my internal medicine residency in Albuquerque, New Mexico, I was excited about the field and excited that I was getting to advance my study and work with real patients. I knew the hours would be tough, but I found myself so engaged in the work that I quite liked the experience, even the thirty-hour calls—which in recent years have been largely curtailed if not ended. I have reservations about this new model, which I think has some negative effects. In fact, one of the big criticisms I have of the internal medicine field is that it's becoming less a profession and more a job. People are getting a shift-work mentality, and there is less ownership of patients.

As an intern, when I admitted a patient I followed him for the first thirty hours. I wanted to know if he got better or worse, I wanted continual feedback. Now, when your shift is over you have to leave; but then you're not there to learn what's going on with him during what could be a critical period.

I'll never forget what the chairman of my residency, a pretty intense individual, told the new crop of residents upon my arrival. He said, "Listen, we have 36 months to take you from being a medical student to being our colleague."

I always remembered that because 36 months is not a long time, especially when you're learning to care for a human being. I didn't want to miss an opportunity to learn, because if I saw something, I could discuss it with an attending and other residents before I made a decision. I wanted to see as much as I could, talk to as many people as I could, so I rather liked long call periods.

I recall a situation where as an attending I had to be up for 48 hours. I was okay with it, largely because I had been trained, I knew what I was doing, I was comfortable in my knowledge—but *that* was because I'd already had experiences being up 30 hours and having people support me in my decisions. Since the new system of proscribed call shifts, I'm noticing a greater emphasis on completing tasks. Residents are not being asked to be creative or innovative like someone in the business world, where those qualities are valued.

Get Directions: Obtaining a Fellowship

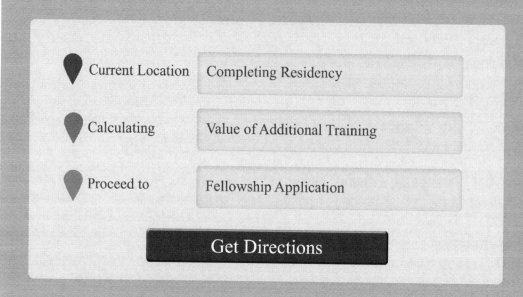

📍 Current Location	Completing Residency
📍 Calculating	Value of Additional Training
📍 Proceed to	Fellowship Application

Get Directions

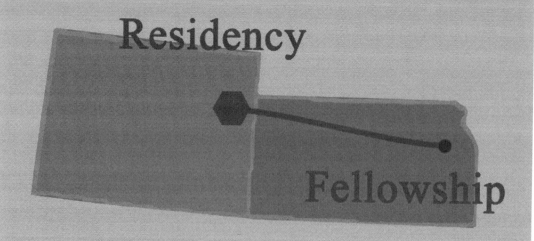

Residency

Fellowship

Training After Residency

"I am in a residency and want to do additional training."

This is always a good idea. With the increase in specialization, gaining a unique skill is a competitive advantage in both private practice and academics. One of the best pieces of advice I've ever been given came from a friend who said, "Never cut your training short by one year."

I was in an excellent training program in cardiothoracic surgery at Washington University School of Medicine in St. Louis. It was only a two year program, however, and realizing that even this school's faculty had done additional training before taking their first job, I committed to go to the Cleveland Clinic for heart transplantation training. Right at graduation, an excellent job offer came up in St. Louis. Since my wife had matched in radiology at Washington University, the position seemed like a perfect opportunity. However, I would have to start immediately and turn down the transplant training. It was very difficult decision, but I turned down the job and went to Cleveland. I had previously learned that your reputation is all you have. Making a commitment to do something and not following through will taint the image you've achieved and negatively impact your reputation. As it turns out, turning down that job was the right choice. I was not ready for complex heart surgery until after my time in Cleveland, where I had an unbelievable experience. Had I taken that job, I would not have succeeded, and I might well have had a mediocre career. Moreover, two years later, that group broke up. I would have been out of a job in the middle of my wife's training. Instead, I landed a job at St. Louis University and built a successful career. The support and training I received at the Cleveland Clinic is more responsible for my success than anything except my hard work and my wife.

To cite a similar example, my wife decided to do a fellowship in mammography at Washington University at the end of her training, after I had accepted a job at Northwestern (where one of my former Cleveland Clinic mentors had taken over). It was a difficult decision and a tough commute. We had two small children but we were able to manage. A few years after she joined me, we decided to return to St. Louis. There were no good mammography jobs in the area, but Washington University decided to create a job just for her.

Work hard, be honest, be positive, do what you say you are going to do, and never cut your training short by a year. As long as it offers a skill set or something to make you more marketable, it is worth it.

AN ALTERNATIVE PERSPECTIVE FROM A CARDIOLOGY FELLOW

The value of serving as chief resident

A chief resident in internal medicine is resident who has graduated and spends an extra year managing the residents in the program. It is considered an honor, and is usually offered to the top resident. In some other fields, the term "chief" means the most senior resident. I did serve as chief resident in my internal medicine program, and while I'm very glad I did, I did not enjoy the experience. Serving as chief did help me a lot in terms of career advancement, but that's not why I took the position.

To backtrack, I found I was quite interested in medical education. I really liked the way I was taught in the UMKC program, and truly believe it's the best way to teach medicine. The students were always excited because everything was new to them, and I really liked the interface we had with professors and residents there. I thought it would be interesting to play a role in improving student education, and that's why I decided to be a chief resident in internal medicine.

The position adds an additional year to your training, but you're more of an attending, and not really a resident. I had my own services, and I had a lot defined duties like taking care of the schedule and other administrative tasks. The chief, as the position was explained to me, entailed three components. The primary responsibility was for the education of the house staff as well as the medical students. The second component was administration, and the third was serving as an attending on all the services. I went into it thinking that my time would be divided equally across the three domains, but found that I spent 80 percent of my time in administration. I was always going to meetings, and then meetings to get ready for meetings, and there was lots of paperwork. Not what I thought it would be!

If you're planning a career in academic medicine, I think that serving as chief is definitely something to consider. It's a good thing to take the one year appointment and learn what it is that academic people do so that you can then make other decisions. I learned a lot in that year, but realized I really want to orient my work in future toward teaching, and limit my administrative responsibilities. Some people are absolute naturals for the more administrative end of things, in which case serving as chief resident is a good move.

The value of a fellowship

A fellowship is required in many specialties; certainly in my field where being a board certified cardiologist is mandatory. In the old days, you came out of internal medicine and then were kind of grandfathered into cardiology. But now that internal medicine includes so many specialties, the extra training of the fellowship is essential.

Get Directions: Obtaining a Fellowship

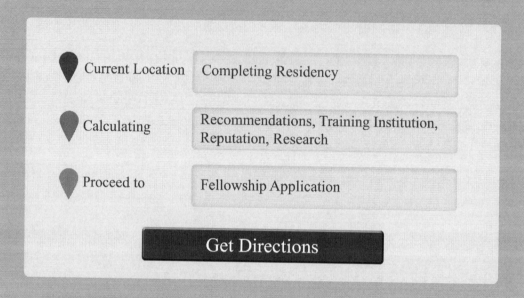

Current Location — Completing Residency

Calculating — Recommendations, Training Institution, Reputation, Research

Proceed to — Fellowship Application

Get Directions

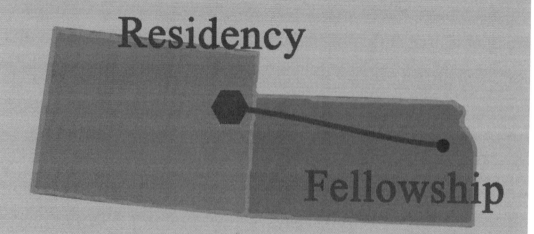

Residency

Fellowship

Tips for Obtaining a Fellowship

"Where should I go and how should I get there?"

This is probably the easiest step of all, and I have some tips for making it successfully.

Choosing a fellowship program.

1) Choose a marketable niche. Becoming an expert in a field that is not marketable is a waste of time, so choose a niche that is being sought after in your field.

2) Choose an institution that has a recent track record of placing people into academics. Even if you want to go to private practice, this is the right decision.

3) Choose an institution whose faculty is heavily represented in leadership positions in your field. If you do a good job there, they will help you for your entire career.

4) Choose an institution with a national reputation. The Cleveland Clinic has been ranked first in heart surgery for over a decade. Even future potential patients appreciate this reputation. You will have a chance to acquire it only once.

How do I get in?

1) Recommendations. They are most important here, and personal connections are critical. Review the section on recommendations for residency. Find

out who among your connections may know the decision maker for the fellowship, and ask them to support you. You have to earn their support, but once you have it, their recommendation alone should help you secure a position, even if you have to wait a year or two for it. When I wanted to go to Cleveland, I asked the one attending who had trained there for his support. I had done the same when I went to Washington University. It does not always work, but a good recommendation from a decision maker can give you your best odds.

2) Research. This is on you. Review the section on research for residency here, as the parameters are the same. This should be part of your job. When your friends are socializing, spend time building your CV. Without publication, research is a waste of time at this point. Choose a mentor who knows how to publish, and look at his or her CV. If he or she does not have a lot of recent publications, seek others and choose more wisely. However, by this time you should have built your skill set to the point where you are an asset and can help the mentor. If you are just a time waster and need him or her to teach you the basics, the experience may be detrimental. If so, you can always look for help beyond your mentor.

3) Reputation of your training institution. There is not much you can do about this now. Just keep working to elevate it. Fortunately, the school's reputation carries little weight compared to the other two components.

Types of Fellowships

There are many different fellowships in every field. In some of the newer areas, for example, robotic surgery as a fellowship is unaccredited and you simply apply to the individual center directly. In some of the more established areas, like cardiology, even interventional cardiology *after* a cardiology fellowship, the application process is more formalized and candidates usually participate in another "match," very similar to the one for residency. That process, while beyond the scope of this book, is easy to identify. Often there is a need for an accredited fellowship in the established areas, as accreditation will be required for board certification in that field. For example, the American Board of Thoracic Surgery tests and certifies graduates, as well as retests and recertifies practicing surgeons. Completion of a certified training program in cardiothoracic surgery, as well as the completion of a certain number of cases must be met prior to examination. Typically hospitals require board eligibility for privileges but give a practicing physician a few years to complete boards. Without completion of boards, many hospitals will no longer let a physician practice at their facility. There is no certification process for a field like robotic cardiac surgery to date. Regardless of the type of training, the suggestions for choosing a program and how to get there remain the same. Identify the pathways for your potential fellowship in the *beginning* of your residency training, and start working on the process.

Get Directions: Successful Private Practice Career

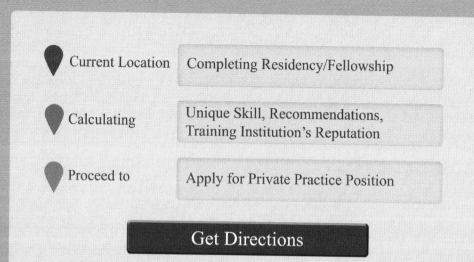

Current Location	Completing Residency/Fellowship
Calculating	Unique Skill, Recommendations, Training Institution's Reputation
Proceed to	Apply for Private Practice Position

Get Directions

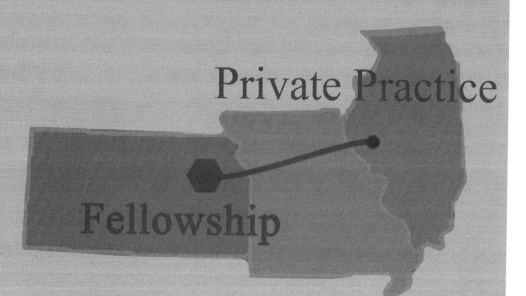

Private Practice

Fellowship

Choosing Private Practice

To a large degree, successful careers in both academic and private practices hinge on the same core elements. One significant difference, however, is that private practice focuses on the clinical aspects of being a physician. Successful entry into the field will depend largely upon the candidate's ability to offer a unique skill to the practice, some expertise no one else in the practice currently has. The bottom line is that the skill will increase the practice's volume.

Every fall, the cycle of jobs for new graduates occurs. Everyone knows that there will be new grads available in July. Often graduates of a program reach out to that program director and ask if he or she has someone graduating that the program director can endorse. If you had a successful training experience, it will be you. Also, the "top" residency programs also receive many similar requests. However you can be proactive, too. If you are interested in a particular practice or region, reach out to those practices in the beginning, middle and end of your residency. If you contact them several times, you are likely to be on their mind. Have people who support you call those practices to endorse you, particularly if there is a connection between the mentor and a member of the group. Be clear that you *want* the job. I prefer to hire people who demonstrate a strong interest in the position that I am offering rather than individuals who present themselves as a commodity that I am "lucky" to have.

These outcomes are largely determined by decisions you make about "direction" long before you get to your first job. Similarly, the habits we've discussed in previous chapters, formed early and refined over your medical education, will most certainly help you achieve your private practice goals. That said, by the time you approach the end of your residency or fellowship and begin to consider your first job, you will face several directional choices. The most important of these pertain to location, practice size, and practice compatibility.

The choice of location generally means choosing between underserved areas, and sufficiently or over served areas. Underserved areas usually are socioeconomically poor, are frequently in rural areas, are frequently in "undesirable" areas, and generally have a relative lack of cultural and educational amenities. Reading this, who would want to practice in an underserved area?

There is no right answer here. The reasons to choose an underserved area are primarily related to the fact that they are underserved. Your career will take most of your waking hours for many years. I believe many of the doctors who choose to practice in underserved areas do so because they want to serve where they are needed and can make a difference. In Boston or New York City, a subspecialist or even a generalist will never be missed from a service point of view. Sure, you may be more astute than the other hundred or even the other thousand doctors in town working in your chosen field. But the chances are high that you will not make a lasting impact in your community, as there are already enough doctors in these cities. Locating in a large metropolitan area where living costs are high and competition likely higher means you will spend many more years establishing a patient base, and encounter more difficulty making a living. There is no right answer, because these disadvantages need to be weighed against multiple other factors that include personal lifestyle preferences (urban vs. country living, for example) and the availability of educational and cultural amenities that will meet your needs and those of your spouse and children.

Underserved areas offer greater access to patients in need of care, and patients are often more appreciative as well as less "high-maintenance." It takes a lot of introspection as well as location research to make the right decision for you. Start by asking yourself some pointed questions. "Is the rural town really underserved in my specialty? To what degree has managed care penetrated the area? What kind of hospital and ancillary medical service support can I expect? Can my spouse find a job? What about schools, religious and ethnic commonalities? What support and resources will I find for family hobbies and interests?"

Practice size is another factor to consider as you look for your first job, as there are tremendous differences between starting a solo practice, working for a small group, and working for a large group.

Let's start with solo practice. Solo practitioners have become much rarer over the last fifty years, perhaps due to the many disadvantages they encounter. There is no senior partner, or even junior or equal partner with whom to discuss patient management. There is no partner to share costs, no partner to share risks, and no partner to share call. You have to run a business, which can be time-intensive, and further, there is no one to teach you how to run one. There are no economies of scale to use in paying for equipment, disposables, your facility or staff.

There is really just one advantage to a private practice, and for the solo practitioner that one reason outweighs all the disadvantages: you are the sole decision maker, a.k.a., the boss.

Most physicians end up working for group practices, but even in this sphere, significant difference between small single-specialty groups, and large multi-specialty groups exist. The small groups are more intimate, while large groups, which can command greater economies of scale in purchasing and contract negotiation, tend to be more bureaucratic and impersonal. Today's trend is toward large groups, even in underserved markets.

Practice compatibility is another decision to be made when interviewing for your first job out of training. Once you determine location and practice size, you will encounter multiple practice opportunities. This is where practice compatibility comes in. Assessing this component is much more art than science, and not much different from picking a spouse. In fact, this choice is almost as important as you will spend just as much time with your new colleagues as you may with your spouse, and divorces can be just as emotionally and financially painful (or so I have heard). The bottom line is simple. Are these physician partners people you want to work with for multiple decades? Are they nice, are they ethical, are they fair, are they people you would choose to befriend? It is clear to me that the answers to these questions are much, much more important than the first year guarantee number that so many doctors get hung up on. Be sure to evaluate other aspects of practice compatibility carefully. Is the partnership track reasonable, or are you comfortable on the associate track? Is the practice run the way you would like to run a practice? Are the patient care metrics (time, resources, and outcomes available to patients) reasonable? Like today's marriage rates, more than fifty percent of first jobs do not work out long term. The best thing you can do is stack the odds in your favor by choosing the correct direction for you, in terms of location, practice size, and practice compatibility.

After these considerations, when you accept a job, it is critical to be successful. There are several tips that may help.

Clinical. The common denominator of any successful practice is that your patients *always* come first. Nothing takes a higher priority. Your clinical reputation is critical, so manage it actively. Don't be afraid to ask for help from a senior partner on a tough patient. Often one or two bad outcomes are difficult to overcome, especially when they occur at the early stage of your career. However with the help of a senior partner, such incidents can be managed. Not being available to your patients is inexcusable; it is also a professional deficit that can never be overcome. I tell my patients that I will treat them as I would a relative, and I always do.

Here are a few tips to help you hone your clinical abilities:

a. Observe the Three As: be Able, Affable and Available. I have been on my cell phone at every family gathering and every sporting event imaginable. It actually doesn't interrupt much.

b. Market yourself as the local/regional expert.

c. Arm yourself with two or three "canned" talks, and contact the personnel office of the hospital you're currently working in to set up meetings with potential referring doctors.

d. Be available to take patients 24/7.

e. Communicate, communicate and communicate.

f. Become an integral member of the community. While networking with community leaders, you will likely be often asked medical advice. When they need a doctor, it is likely going to be you.

g. Stay current. Too often, private practitioners are isolated from evolving practice guidelines and techniques. Every society has conferences annually and often industry provides training courses for new techniques. Take advantage of them. My practice has changed significantly over the last decade. If I was only equipped with the skills and knowledge that I had when I finished training, my practice would be struggling instead of thriving.

h. Be on your best behavior publically. Excessive drinking, drinking while on call, etc., will not be accepted. Behave as you wish *your* doctor would behave in public. Otherwise, bad behavior will come back to hurt you and can even destroy your career.

While utilizing these tips will help you succeed in private practice, keep in mind that over-all career success is ultimately measured by many metrics, including patient volume, patient outcomes, reputation among patients, reputation among colleagues, money, hours worked, and of course the general level of satisfaction and happiness.

If you have a dispute with your partners or hospital, if you have a successful practice with a large patient base, either you will win the dispute or be able to get a better position elsewhere. If you have an unsuccessful practice, you will not have many options during times of dispute.

Although there are several other aspects to a private practice career, from serving on hospital committees to becoming a service chief at a hospital to moving into hospital administration, there is no primary pathway. For pursuits beyond a basic successful private practice career, I recommend that you identify a mentor who has already done the things you wish to do in the future.

Get Directions: Successful Academic Career

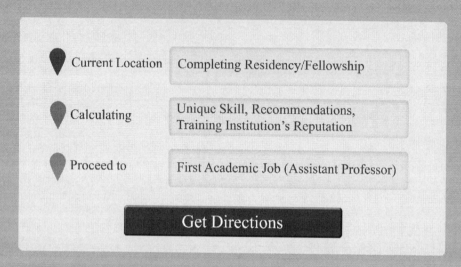

Current Location	Completing Residency/Fellowship	
Calculating	Unique Skill, Recommendations, Training Institution's Reputation	
Proceed to	First Academic Job (Assistant Professor)	

Get Directions

Assistant Professor

Fellowship

Entering Academic Practice

An academic practice shares many similarities with a private practice. Your first job depends mostly on what you offer and who supports you, which is why it is critical to train at the most reputable institution that you can. Just like private practice, most teaching institutions want a clinical skill that will add value to the practice. In cardiac surgery, for example, that could be in transplant, ventricular assist devices, percutaneous and minimally invasive valves or atrial fibrillation surgery. In interventional cardiology, it could be the ability to treat peripheral vascular disease. In cognitive disciplines it could be an expert knowledge or experience treating patients with a specific disorder. Whatever the skill, its value is the degree to which it will *increase* the volume of the practice. Once you obtain a position, there are generally four stages to the top, each occurring over a five–to–ten year interval. These stages include assistant professorship, associate professorship, professorship, and division/department chairmanship. Some individuals start as a clinical instructor. This is a step between a residency or fellowship and an assistant professorship. Such a position is not uncommon, but is usually a planned 1-2 year interval similar to an extension of training. The clinical instructor usually acts as an attending clinically, but needs some time to build a curriculum vitae to justify a position as an assistant professor. We will not address this specific position here. Further, not everyone will want to advance through all the stages. Relocation is often required and the "destination" position may not be desirable for all academic physicians. Not everyone wishes to head a department. However, I will address each of the stages here to offer guidance to those readers considering the entire academic path.

An academic position is comprised of four facets: clinical, research, education and administration. While building sufficient skills to achieve "triple threat" status is difficult, achieving "quadruple threat" status is nearly impossible. Whatever your skill set, be advised that you'll need to build it gradually over time.

Clinical. As I mentioned earlier, just as in private practice your patients must always come first; their welfare is critical to your clinical reputation. Manage your patient care actively and don't be afraid to ask for help from a senior partner on a tough patient. A bad outcome early in your career, with the help of a senior partner, can usually be overcome. Not being available when your patients need you, not treating them as if they were family, can never be overcome. In addition, avoid focusing on a single niche area at this stage. It is much better to develop expertise in two or three areas, as one may not work out. Upon first starting out I was recruited for my cardiac transplantation skill. Over time, my transplants have become secondary to the atrial fibrillation and mitral valve surgeries that now dominate my practice. Shifting emphases as one gains experience is common and likely to occur several times in a successful career.

As noted in our previous discussion of private practice, following the same few cardinal rules will go a long way to ensuring success.

a. Mind the Three As: be Able, Affable and Available.

b. Market yourself as the local/regional expert.

c. Prepare two or three well-prepared talks and ask your hospital development personnel office's help in meeting with potential referring doctors.

d. Be available to take patients 24/7. I have accepted patients for my partners while snorkeling in the Red Sea. In this age of rapid fire cellular communication, there is no reason you can't.

e. Communicate, communicate and communicate with everyone: patients, colleagues, nurses and staff.

f. Do research in your clinical niche and publish it.

g. Look for a clinical niche that no one really wants. In general, if you are willing to work nights and weekends, most established physicians would gladly let you have those patients. Once you are successfully established over a decade or so, you can do the same.

2) Research

a. Find at least one scientific mentor. While one is probably not enough, four is probably too many. Find individuals who have already been successful and done what you want to do. Make sure that whoever you choose will help you and is not focused solely on his or her career. Also make sure one of them has external funding. Make sure your personalities are compatible.

b. Recognize that all science is multidisciplinary. Develop a "village" or become part of an existing network.

c. Focus on research that enhances your clinical niches. This took me a few years to figure out, but once I did the result was amazing. Once you start publishing on a niche topic, you'll find that somehow referring docs and patients find you. In no time your efforts evolve into a self-fulfilling upward cycle; you'll have more patient cases to publish, and even more will come.

d. Ideally seek start-up funds of $70,000–$100,000 for the first three to four years and include a lab technician or post-doc.

e. If there is a robust clinical database, make sure you have access and statistical support.

f. Attend or organize dedicated research meetings.

g. Attend meetings and conferences of other disciplines.

h. Start writing grants for young investigator awards from day one. They may get rejected, but they come back with advice on how to improve. For a few years, you will be eligible for awards from several sources. These tend to be slightly less competitive and they really help you gather data for later more competitive grants.

i. Write grants for internal funding. All universities have some of these available.

j. Consider working with industry. This used to be a very clear path toward success. I was very successful early in my career with this. However as time has gone on, there has been increasing scrutiny regarding conflicts of interest. Therefore I have personally removed my conflicts. However, early on it may be beneficial to partner with industry, as long as you are transparent and fully disclose your potential conflicts.

k. By years two and three, you should have sufficient preliminary data to write a major grant (usually K series, or society grant).

l. Recognize that "protected time" is any time you are not taking care of patients. If you try to limit your research during any "protected time" you have negotiated, you will limit your success.

3) Education

a. Maximize every opportunity. Every moment is a "teaching moment." Don't squander a single one. Take a few minutes to explain and educate with every interaction. Your goal should not be to give the most student lectures; it should be to give the single most memorable one. Aim to win a teaching award.

b. Recognize that everyone is a student: nurses, residents, medical students, and other physicians. The way you communicate with them may be different, but if you are an expert, you have the opportunity to teach them all.

c. Welcome every phone call. The only phone calls that have upset me are the ones I did not receive. Too often those end up in bad outcomes.

d. Don't be afraid to limit your teaching commitment. Most teaching is not reimbursed, but the person asking you to do it is. Strike a balance.

e. If you enjoy teaching, make it a niche. Do research on it. Choose a mentor. Make it a goal to receive a funded administrative position.

f. Create an educational portfolio. Keep track of all your educational contributions. If evaluations are available after lectures, include them. This is a relatively new concept, but it will increasingly be used to determine promotion, especially for those on a clinical educator track.

Administration:

a. Be very selective with administrative commitments. Only say yes if your chief requests it with a reason in mind, as too often these are under-reimbursed and do not particularly help your career.

b. Consider saying yes to selected committees, especially if a committee helps you build your research and clinical niche.

c. Consider saying yes to committees that deal with finance. Most physicians are incredibly weak in this area, so such an assignment presents an opportunity to develop that skill set. Definitely join the main national specialty societies and submit your research for presentation at the meetings.

AN ALTERNATIVE PERSPECTIVE FROM A DIVISION DIRECTOR OF GERIATRIC MEDICINE

The importance of professional meetings

Attending professional meetings is very important to an academic career, chiefly for the interpersonal relationships you can make. I found socializing at these meetings difficult at first until I began asking significant figures like Nobel Prize winners out to dinner. What I quickly learned was that no one asks Nobel winners out because they all think Nobel winners are too famous to approach; and Nobel winners are often too scared to ask *you*. Eventually I met and talked with about 15 Nobel winners that way. Making a practice of asking people to dinner was not only fascinating, but helped me develop a stronger voice at work too.

AN ALTERNATIVE PERSPECTIVE FROM A CHAIRMAN OF INTERNAL MEDICINE

On the role of a mentor

I think a mentor can be invaluable in helping you find your path and keep your footing as you move along. I was lucky in meeting my mentors early in my training, and they've remained with me all through my life, supporting my efforts referring me to things. Ideally it's a lifelong relationship that begins early, while you're still in training. However, it's not something you can always plan or make happen. Some institutions have begun setting up mentoring programs that assign professors to mentor residents, and while I applaud such efforts, assigned relationships often don't work so well because they're forced. The best mentoring relationships happen naturally, through mutual interest and respect.

On the importance of choosing an association

Another key career step is to choose an association that you judge to be important within your specialty once you finish medical school. This means that instead of having the whole world as your stage, you have one or two associations of people in your field. Attend the meetings and soon you'll find those bodies will be eager to appoint you to committees. Do a good job and you'll be asked to take on another one that might be more significant. From this base you can run a committee here, give a lecture there, then a paper somewhere else—and eventually you build a network of colleagues and connections.

The advantage of the association is that it offers an environment in which to set up your career. It means that instead of sending an abstract to any one of ten meetings, you send everything you write to your association's journal, where it will in all likelihood be published. This helps you compile a body of work that's read by peers. Sending articles out indiscriminately only diffuses their impact, so they don't add up to much. Allying yourself with a good association early on is a good way to build your reputation. It's very hard to become editor of a subspecialty journal without holding a prominent role in a subspecialty association.

On the importance of winning and utilizing grants

The ability to get independent funding is the currency of the realm if you're working for a medical institution; you have to show you can bring sufficient money to produce original research. You can write review papers and so on, but if you're going to write a paper that has real impact, you have to have funded research.

There are actually about six different kinds of grants, and they all come with certain benefits and/or limitations. The most basic is the trainee grant, where someone else gets the grant and you're just the beneficiary of it, able to work in the environment so you can learn the language. Then there are what I call starter grants, awarded by foundations by the criteria of how good you and your mentor are. Smaller K-series awards from the NIH are regarded as mentored awards, meaning the mentor must be named. Association grants, awarded by institutions like the American Heart Association or the America Cancer Society—are called "R-series" grants, wherein you are the principal investigator and the grant is funded or not funded on your merits alone. Collaborative grants, in which you're one of a team of investigators working together, represent the next level up in the hierarchy. Then there are NIH project grants, and other types of center grants, which you should be getting by the time you reach mid-career.

Winning grants certainly enhances your value to your department and institution, because you're bringing in needed research dollars. However, the institution does not get rich from this; in fact research projects cost them about 20 cents on the dollar. The real value that comes with the money is recognition and some capacity by which they can hire in someone to do some teaching, which frees you up for other valuable tasks, including your research.

AN ALTERNATIVE PERSPECTIVE FROM A FEMALE ASSISTANT PROFESSOR

Finding and maintaining a life/work balance

Key for women entering a medical career today is finding a balance between being a good physician and being a good mother. This is difficult to do at any point in your career, but it's particularly challenging during residency. You're always juggling, and while most of us make it work, the one thing we all find is that there is very little time for anything *other* than work and home. You don't get your hair cut. You don't exercise anymore because the one or two hours you might have at night for that are the only ones you'll have with your child. If the choice is between working out or being with your child, you don't work out. Sleep deprivation is a chronic issue because even on your days off, you're tired from being up all night with your children.

It's very important to accept that, in order to maintain a balance between home and work, you're going to need a lot of help. Family can sometimes help, but a lot of the time you will end up hiring people. You just cannot do it all: clean your house, do your laundry, cut your grass, pick up your children—and be your best at work every single day. So be prepared to hire help; you will need it. In our case, our families helped us a lot, but we did hire help as we needed it. We also learned to pare down our lives to focus solely on work and children, nothing else. Given the demands of my husband's specialty—his residency and schedule were much more intensive than mine—he was less involved in childcare than I was during training. But when he was off he was always home.

Balancing the work schedules and time commitments of two medical careers can be very challenging once you are both established. In our case, my husband's career is by far the most demanding; he has to be very involved on a daily basis, which means being available to residents 24/7 and he is. It's not uncommon to get 20 calls in an evening from residents needing help with patients. It's not uncommon for him to be late coming home because he's been delayed in the OR. That I don't face that in my job makes our dual-careers-with-children life doable. Fortunately, I absolutely love my field and my job, but every medical couple has to figure how to choose and maintain specialties and careers. In my observation, most of them do even if it takes them a while, and lot of juggling in residency.

AN ALTERNATIVE PERSPECTIVE FROM A DIVISION DIRECTOR OF GERIATRIC MEDICINE

The importance of balancing career and family life

I think it's important that you marry someone who is going to put up with you, and that applies to women as well as men, and any couple engaged in two intense careers, even outside of medicine. Because the two of you can't go out there trying to be super stars, both of you working 80 to 90 hours a week. Managing this is difficult and requires accepting that one of you probably isn't going to fix things around the house, or even around a supermarket.

Yes, you can hire help, but many more men and women want to look after their own children, and that's very tough when you're working 80 to 90 hours a week. Certainly young people today have to understand that as they make choices. In my case, I love what I do so much that the work and hours do not matter as they might to someone else. But I was very fortunate in my wife, who has been willing to do everything, and put up with me.

Get Directions: Successful Academic Career

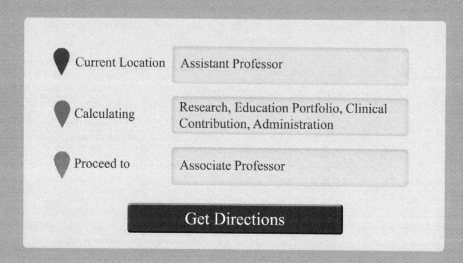

Current Location	Assistant Professor
Calculating	Research, Education Portfolio, Clinical Contribution, Administration
Proceed to	Associate Professor

Get Directions

Assistant
Professor

Associate
Professor

First Academic Promotion

About year five, you should be looking at what you need to do to be promoted. While requirements vary by institution and specialty, in general, all adhere to the same general principles.

1) Clinical. At this point, having achieved two to three clinical niches, you should be building a regional reputation. Earlier tactics still apply, but so do some new ones.

   a. As always stay Able, Affable and Available. This never changes. If anything the value of the mantra increases as you become more successful. If you establish a referral pattern, you can accept patients for your partners. I often accept patients for cardiology and thoracic surgery. I often accept transfers while on vacation and have my partners take care of the patients when they arrive. It does not matter if I am "on call" or not.

   b. Partner with local centers of excellence. For example, I am currently building on our stroke network and reaching out to emergency rooms that already send us patients.

   c. Continue outreach talks, focusing on specific patients that you have personally treated with good outcomes. Encourage your referring doctors to introduce you to others.

   d. Identify a need they have and meet it. Study an area they're currently satisfied with and tailor your expertise to better serve needs they may not recognize. Become a "one phone call" destination.

e. Make it easy for referring docs to reach you; make it painless for them to send you a patient. I usually take down the information and have my office do all the work.

f. Communicate, communicate and communicate. Develop a "wow" communication strategy. This can be a phone call after every patient interaction to the referring physician, or a summary that includes pictures or articles. A word of caution: in this era of advanced technology, make sure that the patient information is always protected.

g. Do research on your clinical niche; publish and present it at both local and national meetings.

2) Research

a. Start to become a mentor to students and residents, but don't spoon-feed them. Identify individuals who come with some experience and help them develop into contributors. If you have to start from Stage 1 with each student, you will not be productive. In fact, redoing every task a student performs will only decrease your efficiency. Better would be just doing the task yourself. However, if you find the right individuals, you can assemble a team that is able to learn, adapt and perform through various rotation stages, will increase your productivity.

b. Obtain an extramural grant (NIH, society grant).

c. Narrow research on your clinical niches. Likely one or two of your niches will be more successful. Focus and develop the winners.

d. Publish. At this point, though requirements are institution specific, you should have published roughly 20 to 30 peer reviewed papers in order to be promoted to Associate Professor. In addition to quantity, be sure to focus on first authorship and the quality of journals.

e. Consider working with industry. At this point, you should have established enough of a clinical niche to partner with industry and become a local principle investigator (PI) in multicenter trials within that niche.

f. Recognize that "protected time" is any time you are not taking care of patients. Limiting your research during any "protected time" you have negotiated will limit your success.

3) Education

a. Every moment is a "teaching moment," so maximize every opportunity to share your knowledge. Start to teach other younger faculty in your department, as well as faculty in other specialties. Take a small amount of time on the weekends to educate when you round. It goes along way. Direct the trainees to become self-educators and follow-up on the tasks that you assign.

b. Work towards a leadership position in education (clerkship director, assistant program director, medical student rotation supervisor). I found that serving as Assistant Program Director was a good use of time. I was also on the Admissions Committee for a decade, though in hindsight this was probably too long. Ideally I'd have stopped this after my personal education and development on it had plateaued.

c. Publish on the educational aspect of your niche. I am currently publishing on surgical simulation. With a little extra work, you can publish on what you teach in a scientific journal.

d. Work to obtain funding for your research in education. I have recently received a small grant for surgical simulation. Funding for education is available.

4) Administration

a. Local. Look for committees that will help you gain experience or influence for your department/division. That I am on my institution's peer review committee helps me manage potential problems with my faculty proactively. I can identify and correct potential behaviors that would otherwise eventually lead to peer review consequences. Again, I strongly suggest that you consider obtaining experience with finance. Identify and meet someone on the promotion and tenure committee to help review you applications so that when you apply you will be ready.

b. National. Volunteer for national committees in societies. Don't be afraid to tell your mentors exactly what you would like for them to do for you, i.e. nominate you for a committee. Don't be afraid to reach out to leaders and introduce yourself and volunteer to help. A word of caution. Academic medicine is not like baseball. In this league, it's *one* strike and you're out! It is okay to decline a committee invitation if unsolicited, but not often, or the askers will stop coming. However, if you accept, do a stellar job. Be the first to complete the review or task and do it better than everyone else. This is difficult as there are a great many smart, hardworking people competing with you. However, hard work well done is rewarded. I have been invited to serve on the editorial boards of both of the elite journals in our field. This is an opportunity rarely given to someone my age, but in this case was based solely on my performance. While "who you know" becomes much less important than "what you do" at this stage of your career, most promotion committees still require that you have letters from people in the field who do not know you clinically. This is where "who you know" outside your institution can be very useful.

AN ALTERNATIVE PERSPECTIVE FROM AN EDITOR OF GERIATRIC MEDICINE JOURNAL

The path to journal editor

I started doing research in medical school. By the time I finished my residency I had published forty-odd papers. That won me some notice. Early on I made sure I got on the boards of several different journals. While at UCLA I became pretty well known for my research work, through which I got to know the editor of a well-known geriatrics journal who appointed me associate editor while he was there.

Then I applied to several others several others in the field. With the first one, I took the impact factor from nothing to the best in the field in a short time. Then did the same with the second journal and when the third, a totally useless journal that had no impact factor at all, became available, I thought well here is a challenge. By that time I'd edited 15 to 20 books, so they gave me the job and I've since taken this journal from nothing to one of the most important in geriatrics.

Two different kinds of people tend to edit these journals. There are those who are very precise and spend all their time making sure every word is right and every comma in place, and then there are those whose skill set is attracting high quality researchers and writers who produce high quality articles. I've made enough friends around the world that I've become skilled at convincing them that my journal is the clear choice in placing their work. So I've gotten a lot of articles that should have gone to JAMA, a feat that allows you to build a very strong journal.

If you want to build a good journal, you've got to build relationships and get people to give you their best work. Of course pursuing your own research is a given. My science, typically, is ten years ahead of everyone else's. I've published about 140 papers by now, so you understand that I love writing. It's all about having fun.

Get Directions: Successful Academic Career

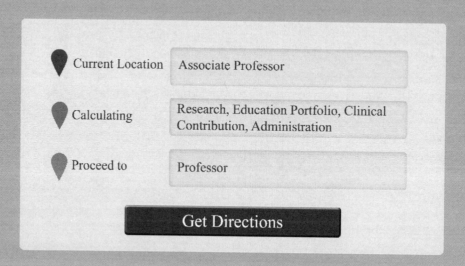

Current Location	Associate Professor
Calculating	Research, Education Portfolio, Clinical Contribution, Administration
Proceed to	Professor

Get Directions

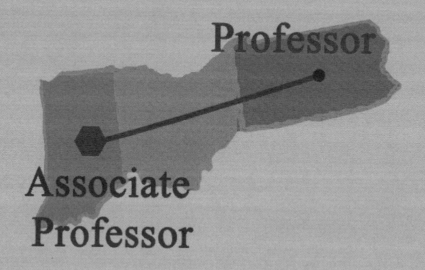

Professor

Associate Professor

Promotion to Professor

About year ten, or about 5 years after you have been an associate professor, you should be looking at what you need to be promoted to professor. Sometimes it comes sooner, usually later and sometimes not at all. Each institution and specialty varies, but the same general principles apply.

1) Clinical. At this point, you should have at least one clinical niche with a national reputation and should be working on a second. There are clearly life cycles to every treatment and procedure. Try to stay on the cutting edge of a few.

    a. Continue to mind the Three As: Able, Affable and Available.

    b. Become a clinical mentor to your junior colleagues. Help them develop their niches, refer some of your patients in that niche to them and be available to give advice.

    c. Continue outreach efforts and work with junior faculty to go together. Let them build on your reputation.

    d. Communicate, communicate and communicate. Maintain your "wow" communication for the department based on your previous work for your individual practice.

    e. Become a national expert in at least one clinical niche. What that is depends on your training, your experience and your local environment; it is your job to figure that out.

2) Research

    a. Become a mentor to junior faculty members. Allow them to integrate into your niche and take it in a new direction.

    b. Help your mentees obtain grants.

    c. Continue to obtain your own grants

    d. Publish. At this point, for a promotion to Professor, you should have at least 50 peer reviewed papers, but again this is institution-specific. Some may require more or may require "high impact" journals. Make sure you are the senior author on at least half of your publications.

    e. As in previous stages of your career, consider working with industry. If at this point you do, work to become a national PI in multicenter trials in your niche.

    f. Protect your "protected time." Any infringement on time you've designated for research, however well intended, will limit your success.

3) Education

    a. Welcome and maximize every opportunity to teach, both other younger faculty in your field and faculty in other specialties. Initiate a course or an award to inspire excellence in teaching. Recognize other faculty when they excel in instruction.

    b. Obtain a leadership position in education. This is a good time to begin running a residency program as director or an equivalent position in the medical school.

    c. Publish on the educational challenges you encounter in your niche, and mentor junior faculty in every aspect of teaching it.

    d. Obtain funding for your research in education and/or an educational program.

e. Develop and direct an educational program for local physicians.

f. Serve on national educational committees.

4) Administration

a. Local. Look for committees that will help you gain experience or influence within your department/division. Place and encourage other faculty to apply for committee service that will be helpful for your department. Be a team player. The person who tries to take all the credit usually eats alone and has limited success.

b. National. Develop alliances with other national academic players. Work together on research projects and society projects. Earn the respect of others in the field and aim for a leadership position in one of the societies.

Get Directions: Successful Academic Career

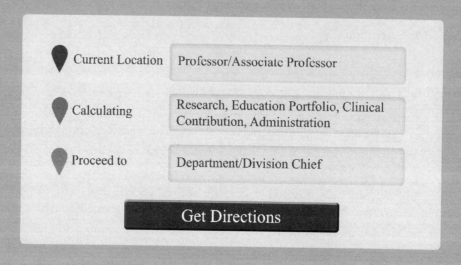

📍 Current Location	Professor/Associate Professor
📍 Calculating	Research, Education Portfolio, Clinical Contribution, Administration
📍 Proceed to	Department/Division Chief

Get Directions

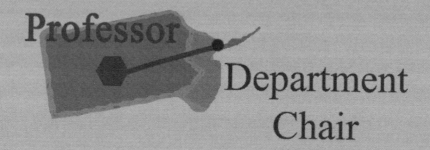

Professor Department Chair

Division Chief/Department Chair

By year 15, you should decide if you wish to run a program or not. Most people don't. I did. Sometimes you will be happy with your institution and will not want to leave, but there will be no opportunity. At times the structure of an institution will make your background appropriate for a division chief position; sometimes it will be appropriate for a department chief. For example, in many institutions, gastroenterology is only a division. A GI physician may or may not be eligible for a department chairmanship depending on the history of the institution. Often, a move is required for this opportunity.

Generally, experience counts. It is easier to get a chief job if you have one already. While doing two years of research in my residency, I acquired an MBA degree, which gave me excellent preparation as well as experience with finances. I also chaired the blood bank committee, which had an annual budget of 10 million dollars. All such experiences in leadership positions will help you build a convincing case for your consideration as a candidate for a chairmanship.

1) Clinical. At this point, you are recognized as a national expert in at least one niche.

   a. Continue practicing the Three As: Able, Affable and Available.

   b. Become a clinical mentor to your junior colleagues and teach the other more senior colleagues how to mentor others. Help them develop their niches, refer some of your patients to them in that niche and be available for advice.

   c. Continue outreach efforts and work with junior faculty to go together. Let them build on your reputation.

163

    d. Communicate, communicate, and communicate, especially concerning the vision and finances of the department to the faculty.

    e. Recognize that in the past, your success was judged by your clinical practice and outcomes. Now you are judged on the success and volumes of the entire program. You can't carry it all on your back. While you will do most of the heavy lifting, you will also need to motivate others to lift as well.

2) Research

    a. Mentor junior faculty. Allow them to integrate into your niche and take it into a new direction.

    b. Motivate and incentivize other faculty to become mentors.

    c. Focus on the number of grants being generated in the department and find ways to increase them.

    d. Track and focus on the number of publications within the department, and find ways to motivate and incentivize the faculty to maximize production.

    e. Track and increase the number of clinical trials within the department and motivate and incentivize faculty to increase them.

    f. Recognize that there is no protected time.

3) Education

    a. Maximize every opportunity. Every moment is a "teaching moment," so don't squander a single one. That includes teaching your faculty. Develop a culture of excellence.

    b. Obtain a leadership position in education within the medical school and develop other faculty members' educational leadership.

    c. Publish on the educational aspect of your niche and mentor multiple faculty colleagues in this niche.

d. Track and increase the department's educational funding.

e. Develop and direct an annual educational program for local physicians that highlight your faculty's skills and niches.

f. Chair national educational committees and recommend deserving faculty for appointments.

4) Administration

a. Local. Look for committees that will help you with experience or influence for your department/division. Place and/or encourage other faculty members to apply for committee service that will be helpful for your department.

b. National. Earn the respect of others in the field and aim for a leadership position in one of the societies. The ultimate goal is to become a president of one of these societies. Achieving this particular goal is difficult, and often related to factors that are beyond your control. However, with hard work you can become a leader in the field and create opportunities for deserving faculty.

Afterward

Get Directions presents the steps to achieving a successful career in medicine. As you've seen, the path really does begin in high school, though it doesn't have to. You can enter at multiple points in the beginning, and correct your course at any point along the way when you encounter obstacles, miscalculations and mistakes. But no matter where you begin your journey, or how many detours you make, every path you follow will merge into the same sure route—as long as you have a passion for medicine and helping others. *Get Directions* is by no means an exhaustive compilation of all the steps necessary to achieve that dream. Rather, it is meant to serve as an informative, insightful and accessible roadmap to young people wishing to pursue medical school. The journey must be yours alone. While I sincerely hope the guide's directions help, every journey is unique and only you can find your way. I can promise you, however, that no matter where or how you get there, the rewards of career in medicine are greater than any other. I hope you get the opportunity to realize them as I have.

Made in the USA
Charleston, SC
11 July 2015